RAISING
HEALTHY
TEENAGERS

RAISING HEALTHY TEENAGERS

Equipping Your Child to Navigate the Pitfalls and Dangers of Teen Life

THOMAS KERSTING

BakerBooks
a division of Baker Publishing Group
Grand Rapids, Michigan

© 2023 by Thomas Kersting

Published by Baker Books
a division of Baker Publishing Group
PO Box 6287, Grand Rapids, MI 49516-6287
www.bakerbooks.com

Printed in the United States of America

Library of Congress Cataloging-in-Publication Data
Names: Kersting, Thomas, 1972– author.
Title: Raising healthy teenagers : equipping your child to navigate the pitfalls and dangers of teen life / Thomas Kersting.
Description: Grand Rapids, MI : Baker Books, a division of Baker Publishing Group, 2023. | Includes bibliographical references.
Identifiers: LCCN 2022018480 | ISBN 9781540900319 (paperback) | ISBN 9781540903044 (casebound) | ISBN 9781493439508 (ebook)
Subjects: LCSH: Parent and teenager. | Parenting—Psychological aspects. | Adolescent psychology.
Classification: LCC HQ799.15 .K467 2023 | DDC 306.874—dc23/eng/20220711
LC record available at https://lccn.loc.gov/2022018480

The author is represented by the literary agency of Park & Fine Literary and Media.

Some names and identifying details have been changed to protect the privacy of individuals.

Baker Publishing Group publications use paper produced from sustainable forestry practices and post-consumer waste whenever possible.

23 24 25 26 27 28 29   7 6 5 4 3 2 1

This is dedicated to every parent who wants the absolute best for their children.

Contents

Introduction   9

1. Mental Freedom   13
2. Social Nutrition   37
3. Fear-Filled Nation   59
4. Behavior and Conduct Issues   79
5. Substance Abuse   101
6. Obesity and Body Image   121
7. School and Learning   137
8. College Admissions Pressure and Debt   155

Final Thoughts   175
Acknowledgments   179
Notes   181
About the Author   189

Introduction

When I was a kid, my mom often said to me, "I wish you could have grown up in the sixties. It was the best." Now, as a father, I often find myself telling my kids, "I wish you could have grown up in the eighties. It was the best."

In the eighties we played outside in the dark, survived mullets and big hair, and walked around town without worrying about being abducted. We rode our bikes to school and everywhere else, took the bus to the mall, hopped in the back of pickup trucks, and traveled in cars without airbags. We had hair-metal bands, arcades, Mongoose bikes, and Ferrari sunglasses. Boom boxes and Walkman cassette players were everywhere, but there were no flatscreens or smartphones. We had Atari and Nintendo but no TikTok or Instagram.

Some of my greatest memories are with my cousin and best friend, Paulie. We did everything together from the time we were born. One summer when we were twelve, our grandmother purchased memberships for us at the local swim club. We rode our bikes there practically every day and were the swim club Wiffle ball champions. After spending most of our day swimming, jumping off thc high-dive, eating French fries, and smacking Wiffle balls over the fence, we'd bike back home, grab our fishing poles, and head over to the small lake nearby.

We were required to be home on time for dinner with our families. After dinner we'd head back outside to play some nighttime Manhunt with our friends in the neighborhood. In the winter we still spent most of our time outside and very little time inside. We played ice hockey after school, made snow forts, had snowball fights, went sledding, and earned money shoveling driveways in the neighborhood.

As teenagers, Paulie and I did what we had to do at school, worked as many jobs as we could after school and on weekends, and spent a lot of time around the fire in the woods with our friends. We went to high school parties, played sports, and were rarely home.

Although there was AIDS, the crack epidemic, and the fear of nuclear war with Russia, we didn't worry all that much because we were more interested in watching *The A-Team*, not the news, and we didn't have social media feeding us fear. Our minds were raw and unadulterated, and that was a good thing. We expected nothing from anyone, including our parents. If we wanted something, we worked for it.

Life is very different for today's kids. Many practically live in a virtual reality and spend way more time indoors, alone in their bedrooms, than they do outdoors with their friends. They digest endless amounts of information, videos, pictures, and other content from their handheld devices, and they suffer from more anxiety, depression, and other mental health conditions than any other generation in history. There are also more overweight and obese kids than at any other time in history. The pressure to attend a "top" college is over the top—and the ensuing debt is even more crippling. The suicide rate is at an all-time high, overdose deaths are epidemic, and young people's thoughts and beliefs are often controlled by media, politics, and TikTok videos.

The question is, What can we do about this? Should we just accept that this is the way their lives are nowadays, that it's just a sign of the times? I don't think so.

My goal in the coming chapters is to inform you, not scare you, about what is going on in our children's minds and lives and why. I'm also going to provide simple strategies you can start to implement in your household so you can prepare your children to go out there and seize the world instead of the world seizing them.

One strategy is to ensure your children have plenty of in-person interaction with peers. Whether they are young children who are play-saturated or teenagers who simply hang out and socialize on the bleachers, kids who are together develop strong social-emotional skill sets. They manage anxiety better, make friends more easily, and resolve conflicts more effectively.

Studies show that children who spend more time outside are happier and smarter, as well as more attentive and less anxious. Outdoor play also promotes creativity and imagination while teaching responsibility for nature. Kids who exercise regularly, whether by riding their bikes or playing sports, have higher levels of self-confidence and enhanced brain structures that lead to higher grades and test scores. They also experience a significant decrease in psychological stress and sleep disturbance.

Parents have the opportunity to be the greatest influencers on children's thoughts, emotions, and lives. Having consistent, meaningful conversations with our children and spending lots of time with them is key. This allows us to impart love and our adult wisdom upon them, providing them with an opportunity to experience lifelong success and happiness.

Children with strong mental health are always happier, more attentive, less anxious, and less aggressive. It opens up their creative imaginations and ambitions and also helps solidify peer-to-peer relations. Finally, kids with robust mental foundations are more likely to be confident, excel in school, resist peer pressure, and lead by example. What more could we want for our children?

Let's take a look into the lives of modern-day kids and try to sort all of this out. Yes, the world around us has changed, but it's time for us to do what is necessary to help our children live happy, productive lives so that the next generation will be better off.

Mental Freedom

When children are little, their parents are often their heroes. This was true for our children. They spent their time with my wife and me playing games, reading books, going to the park, and watching cartoons. They also depended on us for everything, from the clothes they wore to the food they ate to the love and safety we provided.

When children move on to middle school, parents often become less heroic. Middle schoolers prefer not to be seen in public with their parents and would rather be on their phones, with their friends, or by themselves in their bedrooms. When we try our best to communicate with them and talk to them about important life issues, our words often fall on deaf ears as they roll their eyes and respond with one-word answers. Most of them make it through adolescence unharmed, but many do not. There's a lot going on in the world out there.

As a therapist for nearly twenty-five years, I've counseled thousands of kids and dealt with every issue under the sun, from cutting and drug addiction to anxiety and suicide. Being a kid isn't easy. It never has been, but in today's super-charged world I'd argue that it's harder than ever.

I know our parents said the same thing to us when we were kids. Every generation is different, and the world is constantly changing. I get it! Regardless of the different issues that each generation of children faces, the most challenging thing they face is simply being a kid.

Adolescence is hard. It's a natural stage of development with many obstacles. I call it the purgatory stage—a sort of limbo. It's the slow transition from childhood to adulthood during which our children are going through puberty and experiencing hormonal and physical changes.

On top of that they feel insecure because they look awkward, act weird, and are desperately trying to fit in somewhere. They want to be wanted. They want to be noticed by their peers. The good news is that all of this is normal, and in most cases our kids make it through this difficult stage and turn into fine men and women. However, the truth is that the challenges kids face today are so much different from the ones we faced as kids.

Remember the 1970s television sitcom *Happy Days*? It portrayed the stereotypical White, middle-class, American family of the 1950s and '60s. The main character, Richie Cunningham, was a redheaded all-American teenager living in Milwaukee who didn't have a bad bone in his body.

A main setting for the show was Arnold's Drive-In, a standard 1950s teen hangout, the place where Richie and other teens sipped milkshakes, pumped dimes into the jukebox, and showed off their Chevys and Thunderbirds.

In one of the earlier episodes, fifteen-year-old Richie was pressured into joining a drinking game and accidently became drunk. After Richie stumbled home and came face-to-face with his father, he was surprised by his father's reaction. Instead of getting angry, he remained calm. He walked Richie to his bedroom, made coffee for him, and tucked him under the covers. The episode showed the consequences of teenage drinking and offered a strategy for parents on how to handle a similar situation appropriately. It also demonstrated the typical mistakes that teens of that generation made and how they learned and grew from them. In Richie's case, getting sick from the alcohol was the lesson learned.

For me, the best part about *Happy Days* was its depiction of how teenagers socialized in the 1950s and the issues they faced, because it was completely different from how kids today socialize and the things they face. The 1950s kids seemed like they had it easy in comparison.

When I research past generations, it seems like teenagers in 2011, just a decade ago, had more in common with 1950s teenagers than they do with 2022 teenagers.

Why? Because in 2012 our society changed like never before. Smartphones became mainstream, and they have altered the way kids grow up. Although these minicomputer devices and the social media sites that are downloaded on them are designed to connect kids with one another, they have the opposite effect. They create a distance between kids, leading to less in-person interaction, quite the opposite of what you'd find at Arnold's Drive-In.

Teenagers today aren't spending as much time outside of the house as previous generations did. Instead they're spending most of their free time alone, in their bedrooms, scrolling through social media, watching other teens twerk and dance. Or they're playing video games virtually with friends and strangers, or watching YouTube and flipping through TikTok for hours at a time.

According to a study conducted by Dr. Aric Sigman, screen time has replaced outdoor time. Sigman says,

> This report confirms what most parents already know, that discretionary screen time is their children's main activity. Whether watching TV, playing games on laptops and iPads or spending time on social media, recreational screen time is occupying hours of their day, and has replaced outdoor play.[1]

Ultimately, for many children today their sense of reality can be a virtual reality. All of that screen time drowns their brains with an endless flow of shallow content, distraction, and little purpose. If you have a middle schooler or high schooler, you know exactly what I'm talking about.

Yes, I spent time in my bedroom as a kid too, but it wasn't nearly as much as modern-day kids do. I was outside almost all of the time with friends, and I can honestly say that I had a phenomenal childhood. Although we didn't have an Arnold's Drive-In, we did have Friendly's and our Mongooses.

Furthermore, I don't remember any kids in my neighborhood having anxiety or depression or taking medication, and I certainly don't recall anyone taking their own life. However, if you were to ask your own children if they know anyone who is struggling with these issues, they would look at you as if you had two heads and say, "Uh . . . yeah. Duh!"

Yes, every generation changes. The 1950s kids were different from the '60s kids, and the '60s kids were different from the '70s kids, and so on. In my previous book, *Disconnected*, I explored the modern-day screen world that kids today live in and the effects it has on their mental health. Some would argue that it's just the way life is today and, like every other generation, we evolve. Nope! I'm not buying it, and neither should you.

There's something more ominous happening in our world. There's a reason more kids than ever before are suffering from serious mental health conditions and dying by suicide. To understand those reasons, let's explore what's going on inside their minds.

Generation Mindless

First off, what is the mind, and where do thoughts even come from?

Let's say you were born on a deserted island, all by yourself. What would you even think about? You wouldn't know what a milkshake or a smartphone even were. Heck, you wouldn't know what you were. Our thoughts come from the things we experience on a daily basis.

During my own childhood, the thoughts downloaded into my mind came from my experiences on the ball field, the schoolyard, and the swim club. For today's kids, the thoughts circulating in their minds are downloaded by algorithms and screens, and it's happening at lightning speeds. Upwards of nine hours a day of high-octane, highly stimulating images and information are being driven deep into their malleable brains.[2] All of this input shapes their thinking and impacts their emotions. Everyone knows this by now, but there's another piece to it: what they're *not* experiencing.

As mammals, human beings have more advanced brains than the deer eating our flowers or the cow grazing in the pasture, but we also have a lot of similarities. We, too, are part of nature, and we always have been. Millions of years ago we had more in common with that deer in our backyard than we did with modern-day humans. We were outside, surviving by scavenging and hunting. That's how humans are wired. It's how God made us. We weren't built to spend the majority of our time indoors, entranced by social media, "news," and Netflix. It isn't healthy for our brains, our development, or our relationships.

Pause for a moment and think about all that has changed in our world in just the last ten years. I'd argue that the world has changed more in these last ten years than the previous ten thousand years, and it's not going so well, especially for our children. They aren't meant to be isolated from the rest of society and their family members. They're meant to be socially and environmentally stimulated. That's why humans are known as social-emotional beings. When the social part of a child's development is compromised, the mental and emotional parts are too.

Val was a fifteen-year-old high school freshman when I first met her. She was referred to me by her high school counselor because she was failing all of her classes and struggling with anxiety and depression. When I first opened my office door and saw Val in the waiting room, I immediately thought to myself, *Houston, we have a problem.*

Val sat in the waiting room chair, hunched over and clutching a pink blanket. Her hair was dyed bright blue and she had eye shadow to match. A display of bright, beaded bracelets covered her arms in an attempt to cover dozens of deep scars. Fortunately, there were no fresh cuts that I could see, which was the first good sign. It was clear that I had a complicated fifteen-year-old on my hands.

When Val stood up from the waiting room chair and walked toward my office, her shoulders were slouched and her chin was down. I didn't know what to expect. I didn't know if she would even talk at all. She then comfortably plopped herself onto one of my reclining armchairs, looked me directly in the eyes, offered me a refreshing smile, and said, "Hello." We immediately hit it off.

Interestingly, Val grew up in a relatively normal suburban household. Her parents were happily married with successful careers. There was no evidence of abuse, trauma, or drug and alcohol use in the home, and no family history of mental illness. As we got to know each other during our first session, I looked past Val's melodramatic appearance and thought to myself, *This girl seems pretty levelheaded.*

If you crossed paths with Val while walking your dog, you'd probably head to the other side of the street and keep your distance. But aside from Val's wild appearance and demeanor, there was nothing in her language, tone, or facial expressions that screamed "crisis." The alarm bells weren't going off in my head.

After our first session ended, Val departed with a big smile and told me that she couldn't wait to come back the following week. As subsequent sessions evolved, a lot more came out. Val identified as gender neutral and had already been in several relationships, with both girls and boys, all of which were abusive. Fortunately, Val had also become quite social just prior to our first meeting, and she enjoyed spending time with her new group of friends. She also diagnosed herself with ADHD, depression, and anxiety.

Eventually we explored her cutting, gender dysphoria, and other issues, and I began to realize how she had gotten to this place. She told me that both of her parents worked full-time throughout her childhood and that she was on her own most of the time. With that came no restrictions or oversight of her internet or social media use. She said that when she was in elementary and middle school, she spent most of her time alone, viewing anything and everything that no parent would ever allow their child to be exposed to. Things like hard-core pornography, violence, abuse, death, and more.

During the most important emotional and psychological stage of development, childhood, Val was victimized and psychologically abused by the internet. The many hours a day of exposure to the darkest of things during a very vulnerable age led to confusion, attention-seeking appearance, self-harm, and poor self-image. She had little sense of reality because she had lived in an evil virtual reality for most of her childhood.

Green Time over Screen Time

In a September 2020 ABC news article, "Screen Time vs 'Green Time,'" Nick Kilvert, an environmental reporter, outlined the key points from a *Plos One* paper on the subject of green time.[3] He argued that parents are right to nag their children to go outside and play because it's good for their psychological well-being. Although we constantly hear about the link between too much screen time and poor mental health outcomes, there's something more to consider. According to Kilvert, studies found that spending time in nature, also known as "green time," was associated with positive mental outcomes.

Additionally, the negative psychological associations with high amounts of screen time can be offset by extra time spent playing outside in nature. This begs the question of whether or not screen time is the true cause of our younger generation's mental health decline. Could it have more to do with kids spending less time in nature? One survey found that American children spend 35 percent less time playing outside freely than their parents did.[4]

According to Danielle Cohen, a writer for Child Mind Institute, a nonprofit organization dedicated to transform-ing the lives of children and families struggling with mental health and learning disorders, "The national panic about kids spending too much time indoors has become so extreme that the crisis has a name: *nature-deficit disorder.*"[5]

Although this disorder is not currently recognized in any medical manuals for mental disorders, some of the prelimi-nary research shows that a lack of time outdoors has a nega-tive effect on children's mental well-being.[6] Cohen explained that humans are instinctively drawn toward their natural surroundings, and that many twenty-first-century parents would question this theory as they watch their kids express a clear preference for indoor screen time versus outdoor play.

How much so? According to Cohen's research, it's esti-mated that the average American child spends just four to seven minutes a day in unstructured outdoor play and over seven hours a day indoors in front of a screen.[7] Cohen cited recent studies that prove that spending time outdoors isn't only beneficial but also necessary for both kids and adults. Most of the studies agree that kids who play outside have better mental health. They are smarter, happier, more attentive, and less anxious than kids who spend most of their time indoors.

Outdoor play also promotes creativity and imagination, and it teaches kids responsibility for self and nature. "Although nature seems less stimulating than your son's violent video game, in reality it activates more senses—you can see, hear, smell, and touch outdoor environments," said Cohen.[8] It also gets kids moving and gets the blood pumping, which is good for their bodies and good for their focus.

Finally, outdoor play reduces stress and fatigue. In natural environments we use something known as soft fascination, which forces us to ignore distractions that exhaust our brain and instead create feelings of pleasure rather than fatigue. All of the features of modern life—loud noises, distractions, and multitasking behaviors, for example—seem to promote attention fatigue, while spending time outdoors in nature reinvigorates the brain.

Although Val is an extreme example of a teenager whose mind and emotions were significantly affected by spending most of her childhood locked away in her bedroom, hypnotized by the deep, dark web, there are countless less extreme examples that are still concerning. One example is Danny, a patient I started seeing for therapy in July 2020, right in the middle of the COVID-19 pandemic. Danny had just turned nineteen and completed his first year of college. He was your typical friendly teenager who had a girlfriend, lived with his parents, and commuted to college.

22

Danny also had anxiety, though it wasn't a crippling type that prevented him from functioning in society. His anxiety was relatively mild, with little worries and fears that invaded his mind and seemed to feed off of one another.

One of his anxieties was driving. He was uncomfortable driving to unfamiliar places and wouldn't drive on the highway, which is why his parents drove him to his first few sessions with me. I used cognitive behavioral therapy (CBT) to help him reframe his thinking as a way of offsetting the anxiety and panic. CBT focuses on challenging and changing cognitive distortions—a person's thoughts, attitudes, and behaviors—in order to improve emotional regulation and develop effective coping strategies.

Gradually, Danny started driving by himself to my office every week. It took him about twenty-five minutes to get to my office by highway and about thirty-five minutes if he took back roads. He took the back roads at first, but I was eventually able to help him tackle his fear of highway driving, and he began taking the highway to my office.

Danny made nice progress, and by late August he didn't need to see me weekly anymore, so we started meeting every two to three weeks. When his next semester of college started in September, all of his classes were virtual because of the pandemic. His bedroom became his classroom. Once school started, we began doing virtual teletherapy because he was very busy with schoolwork and couldn't carve out the extra time to commute to my office.

Danny seemed to be doing well, but as the months passed, I started to notice a new trend: he wasn't leaving his house at all. He wasn't seeing friends or driving anywhere. In fact, when the school semester ended that December, our sessions

23

remained virtual, even though he now had plenty of time to drive to my office and meet in person.

I suspected that his fear of driving had returned, and I was right. In fact, it had turned into a full-blown phobia. Because he was forced to take classes online and was no longer in the routine of in-person learning and the social interactions that come with it, his house became his new comfort zone, particularly his bedroom. Anything outside of the home now felt uncomfortable and scary.

I worked with him and pushed him to confront this issue. I had him start slowly and begin driving every day up and down the street he lived on. He gradually progressed to driving short distances around the neighborhood. Time was of the essence because his next semester of school was right around the corner, and it would no longer be virtual. That meant he was going to have to drive to school and get comfortable being among other people again. Thankfully Danny followed my advice, and I am pleased to say he is back at school, driving normally and completely free of anxiety.

During the pandemic year, I noticed many others of my patients developing anxieties and avoidant behaviors, things they didn't previously exhibit. One example is a fifteen-year-old boy named Graham. Graham was an amazing kid. He was a straight-A student with a magnetic personality, the kind of kid everyone wanted to be around. He even made the varsity baseball team as a freshman and quickly became the little brother the older players loved.

He was seeing me because he had stomach problems that often made him sick. Whenever he had a stomach episode it would really bring him down, to the point he would become depressed for several days. The stomach issue he had is often attributed to anxiety, and although he didn't show any outward signs of it, my professional experience told me that anxiety was the root cause. Regardless, my job was to help him emotionally manage the situation better any time he had an episode.

All was going well with Graham until March 2021, when he was required by his school to self-quarantine for fourteen days because of a possible COVID-19 exposure during baseball practice. I met with him virtually a couple of times during his quarantine, and he definitely seemed a bit down and was suffering from cabin fever. The Monday he was scheduled to return to school, I received a frantic phone call from his mother. Graham was refusing to go to school.

I arranged a virtual session with him that afternoon, and we explored the situation. He told me that the thought of going back to school was freaking him out; he was in a panic. I knew immediately that his pent-up anxiety had reared its ugly head toward school. I also knew that I had to act fast. During our virtual session, I pushed him. I knew he deeply trusted me, and I explained to him why he was feeling the way he was, and there was only one solution: he needed to push himself harder than he'd ever pushed himself before in order to get to school the following morning.

I even called him the next morning and coached him into finding the strength to plow through his fear. I knew that if he missed another day of school, it would only continue to get harder and could quickly turn into a school phobia. He went to school that day and hasn't had a problem since.

One thing I witnessed firsthand during the pandemic was that it compounded the already troubling mental health crisis in our nation. I also realized that for most of the kids I was counseling, it wasn't the fear of catching COVID that was causing all of the anxiety and depression, it was being locked down and secluded from the rest of society, something that Val unintentionally experienced long before COVID and something Graham experienced during COVID.

Ironically, the lockdowns actually helped Val, because her parents were required to work from home and were therefore able to monitor her screen time and set boundaries. The bottom line is that our children cannot spend the majority of their waking hours in their bedrooms transfixed on their screens and completely disconnected from society. It's unhealthy for their minds and emotions.

Cocooning

When a baby comes out of the womb, what often follows are the loudest, most bone-chilling screams imaginable. For nine months that baby was comfortably tucked away inside Mom's warm belly, and now he or she has suddenly emerged into a cold, foreign place.

In many ways, the baby's response to being removed from his or her comfort zone and brought into a strange, new environment isn't much different from some of the stories I've shared. Humans are creatures of habit, even infants. An unborn baby's natural habitat, or comfort zone, is the mother's womb. Once removed from that warm, quiet womb and brought into the loud, cold world, he or she feels uncomfortable and doesn't know what to do, panics, and begins crying and screaming.

My patient Graham, the one with the stomach problem, is a similar example. When he was required to self-quarantine,

26

alone in his quiet basement, the transition back to the crowded, loud world of school triggered a stress reaction. And it only took two weeks for this to happen. Although he didn't cry and scream like a newborn baby, his brain sent similar stress signals to his body that almost caused him to stop going to school altogether.

Locked-In Trauma

As I mentioned earlier, the mental health decline among our youth started around 2012, when smartphones became mainstream.[9] Although the endless content coming from screens can be mentally damaging, the social isolation caused by the preference for being alone inside, staring at a device, rather than being outdoors with friends is a perfect recipe for developing anxiety or depression. It amazes me how quickly kids can develop a discomfort for their natural environment, to the point where just playing with friends can trigger stress.

A perfect example is a June 2021 piece that appeared on Breitbart entitled "'Locked-In Trauma': Young Children Having Panic Attacks After Playdates."[10] According to the article, after more than a year of lockdowns due to the pandemic, children as young as five were experiencing anxiety, and experts believe that 1.5 million children will need treatment for mental health problems. The article outlines an investigation conducted by *The Telegraph*, which found that children had become frightened of everyday social interactions, fueled by social distancing.

Dame Rachel DeSouza, Children's Commissioner for England, explained that children were having difficulties readjusting to normal life. They didn't know how to make friends

27

or talk to people. One parent admitted that her children had developed a fear of going outside while another parent said that her daughter had a panic attack after a playdate with friends.

A doctor revealed that his emergency ward had seen an increase in the number of children who had self-harmed themselves or overdosed on drugs, with the patients getting younger and younger. Another doctor said that he'd dealt with children as young as ten cutting themselves or trying to asphyxiate themselves, and even one child who was eight years old. The closing of schools, lack of contact with friends, and the stoppage of sports and other activities exacerbated the already problematic mental health crisis that began after smartphones became mainstream.

College students were also affected by social isolation and lockdowns, and the effects may go on for years to come. According to a piece that appeared on DNYUZ, young people's social anxiety has worsened in the pandemic.[11] The piece, which originally appeared in the *New York Times*, shared the experiences of young adults as well as insight and advice from experts. Roughly 10 percent of young adults and adolescents suffer from social anxiety, which is defined as an intense fear of being watched or judged by others.

All of the young adults interviewed for the article were living with some degree of social anxiety. Social anxiety has been a growing problem for many years and was only amplified by the pandemic. Months of isolation have fueled social withdrawal and entrenched young folks in reclusive habits.

One student named Garret Winton detected his social anxiety in middle school and was able to tame it when he started college. During the pandemic, however, he lost control. He recalled one afternoon in May 2021 when he checked his heart rate and discovered it was 130 beats per minute—his fourth panic attack that week. He experienced shortness of breath and saw black spots. He lost all progress he had made prior to the pandemic.

As the country started to emerge from lockdowns in 2021, more and more young people began encountering newfound insecurities, a reluctance to hang out with friends, and a fear of public spaces—things that were a normal part of their lives prior to the pandemic. This is something I now see regularly at my private counseling practice. Even teens and young adults with no prior history of social anxiety began to experience its symptoms after the lockdown restrictions were lifted.

Twenty-one-year-old Nanichi Hidalgo-Gonzales, who was also interviewed for the *New York Times* piece, was a "social butterfly" prior to the pandemic and loved talking to people. She described one experience at a restaurant with friends for her birthday where she felt nauseous and claustrophobic, which are symptoms of a panic attack. Before the pandemic, she was excited about attending college and the whole college experience. After, she felt like she just wanted to stay home because she didn't want to go out and become anxious. Wisely, she began seeing a therapist for her anxiety.

Colleges across the county have been offering more mental health resources because of the growing problem of anxiety and depression. The University of Alabama at Birmingham, for example, asked professors to look out for warning signs of socially anxious students after seeing a 20 percent increase in patients at the student counseling center starting in 2019. Experts are concerned that the growing problem of anxiety will also lead to greater rates of depression, which already affects 13 percent of US teens ages twelve to seventeen.[12]

Lastly, one expert who was interviewed, Dr. Yanes-Lukin, was concerned about youths in particular, because it is during the younger years that social skills are developed, and if kids are stuck indoors all the time, they aren't using and developing those skills and will struggle as young adults.

Another article that appeared on NPR called the mental health crisis among kids a national emergency.[13] The American Academy of Pediatrics, the Children's Hospital Association, and the American Academy of Child and Adolescent Psychiatry penned a letter stating that the rates of mental health concerns among children has been rising steadily for the last ten years, and the lockdowns made it worse. Frighteningly, from February to March 2021, emergency room visits for suspected suicide attempts among girls ages twelve to seventeen rose 51 percent compared to the same period in 2019. Additionally, emergency department visits for mental health emergencies were up 24 percent for children ages five to eleven and 31 percent for children ages twelve to seventeen. These numbers are absolutely startling.

Do you see the pattern here? When humans are alone and isolated, away from social interactions, bad things happen. Too many kids in our world spend the majority of their downtime alone in their bedrooms, on their screens, and this was going on long before the pandemic. This is precisely why rates of anxiety and depression have skyrocketed since 2012.

During the pandemic, those who were most vulnerable, or who already had mild anxiety and depression, were hit the hardest because they no longer had school and other activities to provide them with the social stimulation they needed.

The question is, What can we do to help our children, our young adults, and even ourselves?

Get Out of the House

Ginny and Josh Yurich are parents to five children under age fourteen and live in Southeast Michigan. Seven years ago they noticed a consistent theme going on in the parks, trails, and campsites near them: there were very few children. With such natural beauty all around, how could this be?

They decided to conduct some research and discovered that four to six hours per day was an ideal amount of time for children to spend outdoors. Although this may sound excessive, considering that the average amount of time children spend outdoors is under one hour per day, Ginny and Josh gave it a try with their family and haven't looked back. According to Ginny, "Our greatest times as a family, and my most successful times mothering, almost exclusively point back to these fully immersive nature days, and the benefit after benefit to the wonderful time outside."[14]

1000 Hours Outside is a global movement created by Ginny and Josh that has one specific goal: to encourage other families across the world to do what they did: ensure their children are receiving healthy doses of the great outdoors.[15] Through their blog, they inspire and inform others how to set aside the screens and get outside, as nature play aids children in every area of development: academically, socially, emotionally, and physically.

The Yurichs spread out their four-to-six-hour daily averages of outdoor time over the course of a few days, striving for roughly twenty hours per week, which adds up to around one thousand hours a year. Sounds like a lot of hours, doesn't it? Well, consider this: the average American child spends twelve hundred hours a year in front of a screen. So maybe it is possible.

Get Your Kids Exercising

Dr. John Ratey is a renowned Harvard psychiatrist and author of the bestselling book *Spark: How Exercise Will Improve the Performance of Your Brain*. In his book, Ratey writes about the town of Naperville, Illinois, which created the fittest and smartest students in the nation because of a unique physical fitness experiment they conducted in 2010.

While most high schools include physical education as part of their curriculum, along with after-school sports programs, physical education teachers at Naperville High School also created something called "Zero Hour PE," where students schedule time to exercise before class starts and sometimes even during class. At Naperville, exercise doesn't just happen in the school gym; there's exercise equipment right in the classrooms. In an interview with ABC News, Paul Zientarski, chairman of the Physical Education Department at Naperville, said, "What we're trying to do here is jumpstart their brain." Through Naperville's unique fitness approach, "sophomore Caitlyn Porcaro used to get Cs and Ds. Now she gets As and Bs. She says exercise helps her focus."[16]

Dr. John Ratey and Dr. Charles Hillman, a professor of kinesiology and community health at the University of Illinois, were both interviewed as well. Both agree that exercise makes the brain more ready to learn and is good for attention. In fact, whenever a teacher at Naperville suspected that a student was zoning out, they'd give them a short "brain break" by allowing them to use the exercise bike in the classroom. The results of Naperville's exercise experiment were astounding. Reading scores nearly doubled, and math scores increased by a factor of twenty.[17]

There is literally no brain function that exercise doesn't affect in a positive way. It is also a natural and effective anti-anxiety and antidepression treatment. Whenever we are physically moving, our brains release endorphins, which are powerful chemicals that make us feel good. Exercise boosts our mental energy while naturally relieving stress and tension. It also promotes better sleep, sharper thinking, and higher self-esteem.

Do your children a big favor and get them out of their bedrooms and onto the pavement, treadmill, or trail. And while you're at it, make it a family affair. Not sure you'll be able to pull it off? Remember, the average kid in America spends seven or more hours per day sedentary on their screens. Surely we can get them to carve out thirty minutes a day, four or five times a week, for a little exercise.

Regular exercise is something I prescribe to just about all of my patients, because the brain simply cannot function at its best if we aren't moving, and if the brain isn't functioning optimally, we won't have outstanding mental health. Personally, exercise transformed my life. I attribute everything I've ever accomplished to exercise. It has kept me in great physical and mental shape. I am superenergized and happy almost all of the time, and some of my greatest ideas have come to me while running on a treadmill. I have been at it for twenty-five straight years, and I will never stop.

In short, a sedentary lifestyle with little social interaction is the perfect formula for developing a mental health issue. Unfortunately, millions of kids of all ages live like this, and it's up to parents to do something about it. Yes, the pandemic didn't help, but this was going on long before that. If you have a child who is struggling with anxiety or depression, there are steps you can take that aren't complicated. First and foremost, get them out of that bedroom and into the outdoors. Get them involved in as many sports or activities as you can, or start a family exercise regimen. Above all, get them interacting in person with other kids. You can do this!

CHAPTER TIPS

- Replace screen time with green time. The more time kids spend outside rather than inside, the more likely they are to be happier and successful.
- Monitor your children's screen use. Set restrictions on your children's devices and download a parenting app that alerts you of any inappropriate content your children may be viewing. My favorite parenting app is Net Nanny, but there are plenty of other good ones. Do your research.
- Create family time. Most kids today, particularly teens, isolate themselves in their bedrooms. Put an end to this and make sure your children are part of the family.
- Get your kids involved in the family. Give them chores, make them clean up, or train them to do their

own laundry. This teaches them to be responsible and self-sufficient.

- If your child is on the quiet side, get them involved in after-school activities like sports or theater. The more time they spend with other kids, the stronger their social skills will become.

Social Nutrition

Your children's first experiences with socialization start with you. The rules of your household, your religious practices, and every other activity your family engages in provide structure for your children, starting at a young age. Every moment of love, anger, or sadness, and every birthday, party, or sport your children participate in are social learning experiences that teach them how to deal with other people, handle stressful situations, and adapt in a group setting. The interactions your children have outside the home—whether at a playdate or at dinner with Aunt Carrie and Uncle Joe—help your children separate from you and adjust to the world outside the home.

Once your children start preschool or kindergarten, friends and teachers replace Mom and Dad as their primary source of socialization. During the elementary school years, children learn structure and rules outside the home as they must listen to their teacher and follow specific classroom guidelines. This includes where to sit, how to organize their desk, and the proper place to hang their jacket. When they move to middle school, their peers become their biggest influence as they figure out how to fit in while also staying true to their core values and beliefs.

It is through all of these experiences that our children develop social-emotional skills. Social-emotional skills are perhaps more important than any other life skills because they are the bedrock to success in the real world. According to a 2015 study in the *American Journal of Public Health*, having higher social-emotional skills in kindergarten is related to important outcomes later in life, such as completing a college degree, career success, and positive social behavior.[1] These skills also equip children to understand their emotions while also understanding and showing empathy for the emotions of others. They help build strong, healthy relationships in every facet of life. They're the skills that will help your children deal with stressful work situations and difficult coworkers one day, and they foster confidence, motivation, and success.

Social-emotional development begins at birth. Interactions with loved ones start the process and help children develop and understand feelings. Developing robust social-emotional skills takes time and lots of interaction with others. It's a learned skill. Kids who have a strong social-emotional skill set make friends more easily, resolve conflicts more effectively, manage anxiety better, and resist peer pressure. They're more confident and are more likely to succeed in school. All of these are necessary skills for a successful adulthood.

Free Play

Although there's a direct connection between too much screen time and poor mental health, the isolation that screen time creates also robs our children of the necessary face-to-face interactions needed to develop strong social-emotional skills. According to Stuart Brown, founder and president of The National Institute for Play, "Educators, parents and policy makers should all be concerned at the rapid decline in unsupervised free play for children, which may damage early child development and later social and emotional learning."[2] He explains that moderate to severe play deprivation during the first ten years of life can lead to a host of different issues later in life, such as depression, addiction, poor self-control, and fragile interpersonal relationships. One leading American scholar on the subject of childhood play, Joe Frost, "contends that the diminution, modification and/or disappearance of play during the past 50 years is causing a public health crisis and a threat to societal welfare that may last generations."[3]

Brown's research found that social-emotional skills develop slowly through childhood play. Play-deprived children may not learn the complicated languages of play, which slowly bring together important cognitive, emotional, physical, and social elements that are necessary for personal competence in playing. When play-deprived children have an occasional play opportunity, they often feel isolated or bullied or may become the bully, because they often overdo the play or don't understand what is going on. Regular play activates as many as three thousand genes in the executive part of the brain, known as the cortex. The cortex governs decision-making and shapes the social part of humans.

Brown also touches on the topic of "helicopter" parenting and how this can also affect social-emotional learning. Helicopter parents often orchestrate how they want their children to play, which can affect the child's own instinctive capabilities. Brown believes that when children become highly sensitized to what their parents want to see while playing, they often suppress their intrinsic play experience in order to gain approval from the parent who is trying to mold them. This can cause them to become skilled at pleasing adults and develop conformist behavior, which reduces intrinsic motivations and authentic exuberance on the playground.

When a child is severely play-deprived or the offspring of a helicopter parent, they may often fail to engage in society. Rather than developing a sense of belonging, they may have explosive reactions to circumstances. As adults, they may have little optimism and can be subject to severe depression due to a lack of joy in their lives

Conversely, children who are play-saturated are more resilient as well as more comfortable with and curious to know other children who are different from them. Developing empathy and tolerance are natural manifestations of regular play, says Brown. Parents need to recognize spontaneous play is key to learning important social-emotional skills that are just as complicated as learning to read. The social-emotional learning engineered by social play is fundamental to human survival and is the key to human socialization that is filled with fun and cooperative public ethicality.[4]

During the COVID-19 pandemic, basically everything our children need to advance emotionally, socially, physically, and intellectually was put on pause for a long time. I remember driving past the playgrounds in my town and seeing yellow police tape surrounding them. Children weren't allowed to use the playgrounds or any park because of strict protocols. They weren't allowed to participate in their natural habitat.

When our nation was still trying to figure out the extent and risks of COVID-19, I felt sorry for all of the kids who were no longer allowed to do what kids are meant to do: play. I also remember wondering how this might affect them in the long term. Would it affect their social-emotional skills? Would it delay their communication skills? Would it make the mental health epidemic worse? Would it cause more childhood obesity? The answer to all of those questions is yes.

According to Nick Triggle, health correspondent for the BBC, COVID-19 took a devastating toll on our children. Even though they weren't likely to get seriously ill with COVID and there were very few child deaths, children were victims of the virus in other ways.[5] The mental health epidemic already underway got worse, the development of important skills for babies was harmed, and levels of abuse and neglect rose.

With the closure of schools, activities, sports, and everything else, our children's lives were effectively shut down. Children suffered from isolation, loneliness, and sleep issues. Triggle cited a study published in January 2021 known as *The Youth Index*. This study tracked the well-being of young people ages sixteen to twenty-five for twelve years and found that more than half were feeling anxious—the highest level ever recorded—suggesting that young people were losing all hope for their future.

Infants were also impacted. The absence of baby and parent groups, and the friendships that naturally develop from them, meant the babies of the pandemic didn't benefit from the stimulus of social contact that's vital to their development, says Triggle.[6]

Can you see how important play and social interaction are for our children's overall well-being? Social isolation and empty playgrounds started long before the pandemic. The pandemic just made it worse.

Another thing that wasn't fully considered during the pandemic was the impact mask wearing would have on children. At the time, masks became common apparel, even fashionable, like the clothing we wear. Although mask wearing was put in place to help stop the spread of COVID-19, studies found masks provided little discernible benefit and had an adverse effect on children's social and communication skills.[7] And we know how important these skills are for our children's development.

According to a CNN article, "For young children, the pandemic comes at a crucial time for developing skills important for empathy, safety and more—a phase that some parents worry will be impaired by mask-wearing."[8] Experts felt that mask wearing might interfere with children's natural learning experiences and communication skills because we learn by reading people's verbal and facial cues, and when those are blocked out by masks, children may not be able to pick up on safe or dangerous aspects of the environment and people around them.

According to one experiment outlined in the CNN article, children were asked to identify one of six emotions when shown various photos of unobstructed faces. The children were correct 66 percent of the time. When shown photos of faces covered by masks, on the other hand, they were correct just 17 percent of the time.

The article also talked about how, starting at birth, babies learn how to communicate by observing the faces, mouths, and voices of their loved ones. For children younger than eighteen months, learning how to communicate through visual cues is probably more important for the development of language and communication than through the verbal word.[9]

Now that the pandemic is behind us, the evidence is already piling up, showing that nearly two years of mask wearing has significantly impacted our children's language and communication skills.

When my family first hunkered down in March 2020 during the beginning of the pandemic, my wife and I didn't see our parents or siblings, and my kids didn't see their friends or relatives, for a couple of months. After the two-month mark, I used one of my greatest strengths, common sense. On May 15, 2020, my son turned seventeen and a bunch of cars filled with solo, mask-wearing teenagers came down my street to surprise him with socially distanced birthday cheer. After his masked friends parked their cars, honked their horns, and sang "Happy Birthday," my gut instincts took over. I said to them, "You can all get out of your cars and come on the driveway."

Without hesitation, every one of them eagerly exited their car and gathered on my driveway. And boy, were they happy to do that.

That day I decided to violate the rules of that time. All of the research I read showed that COVID-19 infection was less severe for children, and I hadn't heard of a single, healthy child dying from it.[10] So I told my kids it was ok for them to get together with their friends again, in person. They were so relieved. I wasn't sure if their friends' parents would be on board, but much to my surprise most of them were. I set the precedent that it wasn't only ok for our kids to be together but essential. Of course, I made sure my kids were not around any sick or elderly people, including their grandparents. I figured that if one of my kids contracted COVID and gave it to my wife or me we, too, would be ok, considering we didn't have any underlying health issues. It was a risk we were willing to take.

Self First

I understand the importance of social interaction, particularly for kids, and today I'm glad I made that decision. I also understand the power of silent, alone time. Unfortunately, many kids would refer to this as boredom, so they avoid it at all costs and replace it with screen time. Yet that inner, silent dialogue that we call boredom, when utilized correctly, produces the most important relationship of all, the one with self. There has to be a balance between social interaction with others and silent interaction with self.

In my previous book, *Disconnected*, I introduced the concept of "cyber self-esteem." Cyber self-esteem involves modern-day kids, ones born into our screen-filled, social media–saturated world. Once kids get their first smartphones, which is somewhere between ages ten and eleven,[11] they quickly advance to social media sites that their impressionable brains can't handle. And before you know it, they're spending almost all of their waking hours comparing themselves to others or trying to acquire as many likes or followers as possible.

They're living in a very challenging stage of human development known as preadolescence or adolescence, both of which
are filled with insecurities. They're trying to figure out who
they are and where they stand in relation to their peers. They
believe that getting as many "likes," "followers," or "streaks"
as possible is going to make them happy. Unfortunately, this is a
losing proposition because, as I explain in *Disconnected*, one's
self-esteem can only come from within oneself—not from anything outside oneself. That's why it's called *self*-esteem.

I travel throughout the country lecturing on this important
topic to both parent groups and student groups. Whenever
I give a lecture in an auditorium full of middle schoolers or
high schoolers and get to the "cyber self-esteem" part of the
lecture, I pick out a kid in the front row, close to me, and ask
them, "Who are you?" The answer is predictably the same
every time. They tell me their name.

I then move on to another kid, and then another, and the
answer is always the same: their name. After asking five or
six kids who they are, and always receiving the same answer,
I then request one of them ask me the same question, and
some kid will say, "Who are you?" My answer is something
like this: "I am not Tom Kersting. That is just the name my
parents gave me. Who I am is much deeper than that." I
then say, "I'm a happy, loving, caring, powerful, motivated,
determined, and spiritual being."

I go on to explain that every person sitting in the auditorium is also these things. Some of the kids' jaws drop. Some
gaze at me inquisitively, and some have expressions on their
faces as if to say, "What on earth is this guy talking about?"

The point I try to make to these kids is that in order to
know oneself, to understand the depths of oneself, we cannot

be constantly distracted by screens. This is exactly why boredom can be so painful for a lot of people, particularly young people, because it's quite possibly the first time they haven't been able to fill that space with something meaningless, like videos, photos, or games. They therefore never discover who they truly are, deep down inside. In other words, they don't have a relationship with themselves, which is the prerequisite to having great relationships with others.

Meeri Kim wrote a great piece that appeared in the *Washington Post* in July 2021 entitled "Boredom's Link to Mental Illnesses, Brain Injuries and Dysfunctional Behaviors." She described a 2014 experiment conducted by psychologists at the University of Virginia. The goal of the experiment was to showcase the power of the human mind and imagination.

The experiment was simple. Subjects were placed in a room by themselves with no distractions for roughly ten minutes, alone with just their thoughts. The experiment aimed to promote the sheer pleasure that comes from just thinking. Erin Westgate, a graduate student at the time and part of the experiment, said, "We thought this would be great. People are so busy that it would give them a chance to slow down, sit quietly and daydream for a few minutes."[12]

The experiment was a complete failure. The test subjects hated it and found the experience to be very unpleasant. A twist to the experiment was that the subjects were given the opportunity to self-administer a mild electric shock with a button, and 67 percent of men and 25 percent of women pressed it at least once to help pass the time. One particularly unhappy person shocked himself 190 times during the ten-minute experiment. Ultimately, the subjects in the experiment preferred physical pain over the discomfort of boredom.

Kim's piece went further into the subject of boredom to help unravel its mysteries. She explained boredom's link to mental illness, dysfunctional behavior, and substance abuse. She also cited research about prisoners kept in solitary confinement that suggested long-term boredom advances into depression, apathy, psychosis, and even self-harm and suicide.[13]

The bottom line: humans or animals kept in captivity are prevented from having a normal range of experiences and are unable to engage with the world. When we're unable to have that, we often unravel psychologically and emotionally.

Yes, humans are social-emotional beings. We need to connect with others, but we also need to connect with ourselves, which I believe is just as important. It's a balance between the two. Something that I do each day, and teach others to do, is to reserve ten or fifteen minutes to just sit in silence. But instead of just daydreaming aimlessly, like the subjects in the experiment, I direct my thoughts. I paint vivid pictures of my goals and give thanks for everything in my life, and I make sure to add feeling to those pictures.

I'll guarantee that the individuals in the experiment had never done that before, which is why it was so uncomfortable. It was foreign territory to them. Their minds just wandered into a fog of doubt, fear, and deadlines. But like anything else, if they practiced sitting in silence the right way each day for several weeks, it would no longer feel foreign or frightening. Instead it would start to feel empowering. You see, everything about us is an inside-out thing, not the other way around. In order to love yourself you must first know yourself, which cannot happen without looking within yourself.

All of the other things happening around our children—all of the social media noise they immerse themselves in—distracts our children from getting to know themselves. Screen time is superficial, and it not only takes away important, in-person social interaction but also strips them of their ability to delve deeply into themselves, which is where joy, happiness, power, and success come from.

If you haven't heard of the law of attraction, it is a term that has been written about for hundreds of years and most recently illustrated in the 2006 blockbuster book *The Secret*. According to the law of attraction, whatever frequency your mind is currently operating on is precisely what you attract into your life. Like a radio frequency, our thoughts are also on a frequency. Whatever we're predominately thinking about is what we're transmitting out into the universe, and all of our outcomes are consistent with those transmissions.

If you're transmitting thoughts about what you're grateful for or what you confidently envision in your future, that's what must return back to you from the universe in terms of your life experiences. Conversely, if you're thinking about how terrible your life is and everything that you lack, that's the frequency your mind will be on, which is transmitted out there and returns back to you.

Ultimately, we have the ability to take control of our thoughts, and when we do so, we set ourselves up for a bright future regardless of what is happening in the world around us. The only way this can be done is through work, which is a combination of mindfulness and intentionally sitting in silence and directing our thoughts to our liking. Unfortunately, this isn't something that is taught in school and also isn't something that many children have any experience with.

Instead, they're controlled by their thoughts without even knowing it, rather than being in control of their thoughts. As

I explained in the previous chapter, the thoughts circulating in our children's minds are downloaded for them instead of by them, in the form of social media and other screen happenings.

In order for our children to be mentally and socially balanced and stimulated, there has to be a combination of silent time and person-to-person social interaction. One cannot work without the other. Here's why. Although socialization is necessary to develop strong social skills and confidence in social settings, silent time is also needed in order to bolster self-esteem, which is the necessary ingredient for connecting with others and developing healthy relationships.

The Power of the Subconscious Mind

Just when I thought I had seen it all, I came across an interesting article in the *Wall Street Journal* by columnist Julie Jargon, "Teen Girls Are Developing Tics. Doctors Say TikTok Could Be a Factor."[14] After months of studying patients and consulting with one another, experts in top pediatric hospitals in the United States, Canada, Australia, and the UK discovered that an influx of girls with tics had one thing in common: they'd all been watching Tourette's syndrome TikTok videos.

When doctors in the UK began studying the phenomenon in January 2021, videos containing the hashtag #tourettes had about 1.25 billion views and grew to 4.8 billion by October 2021. One doctor who was interviewed for the article believed the tics weren't tied to any underlying disease but instead represented a functional neurological disorder. In other words, from watching so many videos of TikTok influencers displaying complex motor and verbal tics, the subconscious minds of these girls became programmed to replicate the influencers.[15]

Everything we feel or do comes from thought, and there are two kinds of thoughts: conscious and subconscious. Whenever we pause and become present, we're in a conscious state, which means we get to choose whatever we want to think about. All of these conscious thoughts we create then move into our subconscious mind.

Subconscious thoughts are those that wander around in our minds without us choosing them—the daydreamy thoughts. Everything we experience with all of our senses is processed as a thought and downloaded into our subconscious. These subconscious thoughts determine most of our actions. Although most of the events we experience in life are consciously forgotten, they're never forgotten in the subconscious, and they influence our actions, beliefs, and feelings.

Teenage girls developing tics is one example. Another is the things we fear. For example, if you're afraid of mice, at one time in your life you were probably exposed to a frightening situation involving a mouse. Although your conscious mind might not recall the incident, your subconscious mind will always remember it. Similarly, if you suddenly experience anxiety about engaging in a social situation, it means that something you experienced, whether from the news or in real life, made its way into your subconscious and caused this fear. This fear will continue until you wipe the slate clean and reprogram your subconscious mind. This would require taking time-outs every day to sit in silence and visualize yourself engaging in social situations calmly and confidently.

Your subconscious mind is a memory storehouse, similar to the hard drive in your computer, a place where everything you've ever experienced is recorded. The accumulated power of these experiences profoundly influences your behaviors. If you've ever seen the movie *Rocky*, for example, you know it can trigger intense feelings of determination. If you've seen *The Shining*, it probably sent shivers down your spine. But if you really think about it, you're not reacting to anything that's actually present; you're reacting to images on a movie screen. These images aren't real, and yet your body and emotions respond as if they were.

Did you ever stop to wonder how a few words on a page, an image in a movie, or information on social media can make you laugh out loud, cry, gasp, or giggle? When you mentally separate yourself from your conscious surroundings, the present moment, and become encapsulated in a dreamy subconscious world, you become hypersensitive to images and suggestions and will naturally react to them. You don't think about it; you just react. This is how your subconscious mind operates.

The good news is that when you deliberately induce this kind of dreamy hypersensitivity, through self-directed quiet time, you're training your subconscious to work for you instead of against you. All that it requires is a little bit of effort. It's learning how to undistract yourself by embracing the present moment. From this present moment, you can make positive suggestions to yourself and imagine the positive things you currently have in your life as well as the positive things you want to accomplish.

Can you imagine teaching your children this? Here is an example of how powerful your imagination is. Try this simple test: relax for a moment, close your eyes, and imagine you're holding a lemon. Picture its bumpy, slightly oily skin and bright yellow color. Now imagine taking a sharp knife and slicing into the lemon. Imagine bringing it up to your nose and sniffing that lemony scent. Now visualize taking a bite out of one of the slices.

Wait a second. . . . Are you salivating? Most people do. You haven't even touched a lemon, and yet look how your body is reacting physically just as if you had. Do you see how easy it is to influence your subconscious?

The lemon trick gives you an idea of how powerful the imagination is. The brain can't tell the difference between something you've intensely imagined and an actual image you see before you in reality. Therefore, when you bite into that imaginary lemon, your brain triggers your salivary glands, your lips pucker, and your mouth fills with saliva.

Knowing oneself is similar to the lemon trick. When I'm working with kids who suffer from anxiety or low self-esteem, I teach them about the importance of knowing oneself. I ask them the same question I ask students at my lectures, Who are they? At first they tell me their name. Then I explain to them that improving self-esteem requires daily "self" time, and the only way to do this is to power down their devices and carve out about fifteen minutes per day to close their eyes and sit in silence.

When they enter this silent space, they need to direct their thoughts and focus on all of their wonderful qualities: their character, values, talents, and skills. I also teach them to take inventory of all that they are grateful for. I have them imagine the house they live in, the family who cares about them, and the food they have on their table every night.

Ultimately, I teach them how to tap into the deeper part of themselves so they can learn how to love every aspect of their lives that makes them who they are. Again, most kids don't do this very often, if at all. Instead, they spend a lot of their time comparing themselves to their peers, usually through social media, which triggers a mentality that's filled with lack instead of abundance. When my patients practice the art of controlling their own thinking, over time they become more empowered and begin to understand what it means to know and love oneself.

This is what self-esteem is. And a strong self-esteem is the key to developing strong social-emotional experiences and interpersonal relationships.

Stranger Danger

At some point, our children are going to meet new people for the first time. They're going to go off to college, land a job interview, and start a career with a bunch of people they don't know. For many kids the thought of this is scary. For others it's exciting. Why? Well, it goes back to everything I've already mentioned about self-esteem and social-emotional skills. Both must be practiced and utilized a lot. Strengthening these qualities makes it easier to connect with new people.

A few years ago my family and I went to Disney World in Orlando, Florida. My mother- and father-in-law came with us. My father-in-law, who was in his midseventies at the time, can talk to anyone. Our first stop was Animal Kingdom. We got there early so that when the gates opened we could race over to the newest, most popular ride at the time, Avatar. Although we speedwalked to get in line early, we still had about a forty-five-minute wait. While we waited, my father-in-law struck up a conversation with a woman behind us, and their conversation lasted for the entire forty-five minutes. He did this in just about every long line we encountered. He talked to people about where they lived, their children, politics, you name it.

I share this story because there seems to be a shortage of communicators in the world, like my father-in-law. In fact, I would argue that nowadays most people completely avoid any form of conversation with strangers. It's as if they're afraid of something. Take a stroll down the streets of any major city, and you'll understand what I mean. The streets are filled with people who don't make eye contact and seem to hide their existence by glaring into their smartphones as they walk, particularly twentysomethings. Are they afraid that if they make eye contact with a stranger that the stranger will pull out a knife? Perhaps. Or do their self-esteem and social-emotional skills need some improvement? Probably both.

A recent study in the *Journal of Personality and Social Psychology* found that engaging in deep conversation with strangers, instead of sticking to small talk, improves our well-being.[16] In fact, talking with strangers is more enjoyable than people think. Researchers in the study designed a series of experiments with more than 1,800 participants. They asked participants to discuss either deep or shallow topics with a stranger by asking questions. The shallow questions included typical and cliché small-talk topics like the weather and TV shows, while the deep questions were led by emotions and encouraged the pairs of strangers to share more personal and intimate information.

54

To keep the conversation flowing, researchers also allowed the pairs to think of their own conversation topics. Before each conversation, participants predicted how awkward they thought the conversation would be, how connected they thought they would feel, and how much they thought they would enjoy the conversation. After finishing the conversation, they then rated how awkward the conversation actually was, how connected they felt, and how much they enjoyed it.

Researchers found that by the end of the study, those engaged in deeper conversations felt less awkward, and participants overestimated how awkward they believed it would be. In fact, the participants found the conversations more enjoyable than expected and felt a stronger connection to their partner afterward.

Another outcome of the experiment showed that participants who had a deep conversation with one partner and a shallow conversation with another partner initially expected to prefer the shallow conversation but actually preferred the deeper one after both conversations were over. The study also found that people often imagine that revealing something meaningful or important in conversation will be met with blank stares and silence. However, they discovered this wasn't true. Because humans are deeply social, when we share something meaningful and important, we're likely to get the same in return.

New people come to my office every week, many of whom are middle school kids and teenagers. I can't tell you how many times I receive calls from parents who want to make an appointment for their child but tell me how hard it will be to get their son or daughter to agree to come. I tell them to just get their kid to agree to come for one session and that I'll take care of the rest.

Most of these kids are very nervous because they will be meeting with a stranger—me. But in almost every instance, by the end of our first session, these kids feel great and are excited to come back. They're not excited because I solved all of their problems in one session but rather because they experienced a deep, meaningful conversation with someone, something they didn't even realize they intrinsically craved, much like the participants in the study.

My advice is to encourage your children, starting at a young age, to talk to people they don't know. Obviously I don't mean some stranger that pulls up to them while they're walking home from school. Introduce your children to people you meet or people you already know whom they don't know. This will help them develop strong social-emotional and self-esteem skills, both of which are super important as they progress through life.

It's vitally important to get our kids engaging with other kids, starting at a young age. Play is the best way to do this, because it's precisely what helps them develop those all-important social-emotional skills. As they grow, we must make sure they continue to engage in real-life interactions with others. Too many teens spend the majority of their time cooped up in their bedrooms, all alone.

If you have a teenager, you know exactly what I'm talking about. Isolation causes social disconnect and leads to a temptation to indulge in too much screen time. Finally, teach your kids self-mastery, which is done in silence. Encourage them to take time-outs each day and check in with themselves. They can use visualization and imagery, which will help secure a strong emotional framework. None of this is difficult. It just takes a little bit of effort.

———— CHAPTER TIPS ————

- If you have young children, immerse them in play with others. This is critically important to their social-emotional development. If there aren't many kids available for play, seek out playgroups in your area.
- Teach your children about "boredom." Show them that boredom, aka silent time, is the furthest thing from boring. If your child learns to embrace silent time, which takes only fifteen minutes per day, they will start to understand the true meaning of self-esteem.
- Make sure that your children, no matter what their age, are not spending most of their time alone in their bedrooms. This will stunt their ability to develop those strong social-emotional skills that can only be found from human-to-human interaction.
- Introduce your children to people they don't know. This can be adults or other children. Most children are naturally insecure when they meet someone new, but the more they experience this, the less insecure they will be. This creates confidence.

Fear-Filled Nation

I n 1975, Stephen Spielberg shook the world when his film *Jaws* hit theaters. It grossed $127 million in its first week, the most ever by a movie at the time. And boy, was *Jaws* good. The movie featured a three-ton, twenty-five-foot great white shark that terrorized beachgoers in Cape Cod, Massachusetts.

In the opening scene, a teenage girl who runs into the ocean is tugged by something patrolling the waters below. She then disappears into the silence of the deep waters. The suspenseful music played during the scene was a sign of approaching danger and would be used in each of the shark attack scenes throughout the movie.

After several more swimmers are killed by "Jaws," the town police chief, Martin Brody, hires a local fisherman, Quint, to catch Jaws. They set sail along with Hooper, a young marine biologist. The crew soon comes face-to-face with the massive killing machine. Jaws terrorizes the three men for twenty-four hours, eventually sinking the boat and killing Quint.

The scenes in *Jaws* were so graphic and realistic that the film made the hair stand up on the back of the necks of millions of people, including me. Nearly fifty years later, *Jaws* is still one of the most successful movies of all time, a true classic. Not only did *Jaws* break box office records but also broke the psyches of real people around the world. The summer it was released, people all over the world wouldn't swim in the ocean. Today, millions of people are still hesitant to go in the water because *Jaws* is still in the back of their minds.

Even though I am a veteran psychotherapist with extensive training in psychology and human behavior, I'm still amazed by the impact a two-hour movie can have on so many people's minds—and continues to have almost fifty years later. It shows just how powerful and impressionable the mind is.

Today we live in a world that has gone full digital, and children consume incredible amounts of videos, movies, games, and more, which have the same effect that a movie like *Jaws* can have. The difference is that *Jaws* was just a couple of hours long, while the images our children view are constant. I believe this is part of the reason why children are suffering from record levels of anxiety and other mental health issues. Let's explore.

The Overanxious Child

A recent study conducted by the Stanford University School of Medicine found that in chronically stressed and anxious children, the brain's fear center sends stronger signals to the decision-making part of the brain, making it harder for them to regulate their emotions.[1] The study focused on children between ages ten and eleven who struggled with anxiety and chronic stress, a developmental age when children are most vulnerable to mood-regulation disorders such as anxiety and depression.

During the study, participants looked at two types of pictures, ones that showed pleasant scenes such as someone taking a walk, and others that showed distressing scenes such as car crashes. Researchers used functional magnetic resonance imaging (fMRI) to examine the signals being sent between two parts of the brain known as the amygdala and the dorsolateral prefrontal cortex. The amygdala serves as the brain's fear center, and the dorsolateral prefrontal cortex is responsible for regulating emotions.

The participants were asked to respond to each of the positive pictures they were shown and half of the negative images, and rate their emotional state on a numerical scale. They were then asked to view the other half of the negative images, one at a time, and attempt to reduce any negative reactions they had by telling themselves a story to make the pictures seem less upsetting.

For example, participants could tell themselves that although the car crash looked bad, nobody in the car was injured or killed. After they attempted to modify their emotional reaction, they again rated their emotions on a numerical scale. As expected, the participants reported less negative emotions after reassessing the negative images. However, their brains told a different story.

Researchers in the study found that the more anxious or stress-reactive a child was, the stronger the signal that was sent from the amygdala to the dorsolateral prefrontal cortex, thereby inhibiting the dorsolateral prefrontal cortex from doing its job of regulating emotions. However, the opposite was not observed. There was no increase in the signaling directed from the dorsolateral prefrontal cortex to the amygdala after the child reassessed the negative images by telling themselves stories to make them seem less upsetting. Ultimately, the higher the level of anxiety the child exhibited, the less likely they were to regulate their emotional reaction to negative images, suggesting that the dorsolateral prefrontal cortex was less likely to carry out its job.

Although results from the study revealed that the brain is not self-correcting in anxious children, it did offer some hope. According to Dr. Victor Carrion, one of the study's coauthors,

> Thinking positively is not something that happens automatically. In fact, automatically we think negatively. That, evolutionarily, is what produced results. Negative thoughts are automatic thoughts, and positive thoughts need to be practiced and learned.[2]

I disagree that negative thoughts are "automatic." I think a person's thoughts and how their body reacts to those thoughts have everything to do with their life experiences and what they are exposed to. All of the children in the study lived in a California community with predominantly low-income residents who often faced high levels of adversity. If the children had lived in a higher income community with little adversity, would they have suffered from chronic anxiety and chronic stress? Perhaps not.

Yes, the Stanford study proved that children who are chronically stressed or anxious have a more difficult time regulating their emotions than others. That makes sense. Furthermore, when these already anxious kids viewed a picture of something distressing, they weren't able to work their way through the distress and find calmness. The strong fear signal from their amygdala was more powerful than the "calm" signal sent from their dorsolateral prefrontal cortex back to the amygdala.

If a simple still photo is capable of causing so much distress for anxious kids, do all the distressing images and videos that anxious kids are undoubtedly exposed to on a daily basis impact them? This question was not included in the study.

September 11, 2001, was a tragic day in American history. Two planes slammed into the World Trade Center in New York City, and the troubling event was captured on video and shown all over the news repeatedly. You can go online and find hours of graphic images from that day, even though it occurred before smartphones existed. I can tell you that those images certainly left a permanent imprint on my brain.

Today, nearly seven billion people in the world, 84 percent, have smartphones, which have cameras that take still photos and videos. Furthermore, cameras are mounted on buildings and homes on every block. It seems that literally everything occurring in the world is caught on camera and is instantly distributed to television news shows and social media sites. We see everything: carjackings, murders, crashes, you name it. We also know that kids spend most of their time online, where all of these events quickly funnel to. It's like *Jaws* on steroids. It's fear porn that is never-ending.

Although the Stanford study revealed that overanxious children were not able to regulate their emotions when they viewed a disturbing image, I'd like to see a long-term study in which overanxious kids practice daily mindfulness and visualization for an extended period of time. I believe it would be an effective antidote to their anxiety.

Fear Explained

What exactly is fear? Why do people suddenly have panic attacks during which they sweat profusely with hearts pounding, feeling as if they are going to die? Why would a harmless spider, for example, cause a person to jump out of their seat in terror? These kinds of reactions are part of our body's natural defense mechanism, the alarm system that's designed to protect us from life-threatening dangers. These physiological responses are evolutionary, dating back millions of years to when humans lived in unprotected caves and fought off predators.

Fortunately, we no longer have prehistoric creatures trying to eat us, and if we did, we would have weapons to protect ourselves. But our subconscious mind doesn't know this; it simply responds to what it perceives as hazardous by sending danger signals from the amygdala to the body in an attempt to protect us, even if a situation isn't actually life-threatening. Giving a speech in front of a crowd of people is a perfect example. It is something that 75 percent of people are terrified of, a fear I know firsthand.

My first panic attack occurred when I was in the fifth grade. I was a typical, happy kid who wasn't bothered by anything. Some of my Catholic school classmates were altar boys, and I thought it looked cool, so I decided I wanted to give it a try.

I remember my first—and last—day as an altar boy. I came out from behind the vestibule with the priest and sat by the altar. There were a couple hundred people at Mass, and I remember gazing out at the crowd and feeling slightly nervous at first, nothing terrible. Then my nervousness spiraled into a paralyzing panic. My entire body began trembling, and my heart felt like it was going to jump out of my chest.

I had no idea what was happening, because I had never experienced anything like that before. It lasted for the duration of Mass, and to this day I have no idea how I was able to do my duties. That was the only time I served as an altar boy.

As the years went on, I never gave much thought to that experience until the same symptoms happened during my sophomore year of college. I was late for a class on the first day of the semester because I'd gotten pulled over for speeding. I remember scrambling to find the building and the classroom and arriving about thirty minutes late. I wasn't nervous. I just wanted to get to class.

When I arrived, I entered through the side door, and the professor stopped what he was doing and looked at me. So did every student in the classroom. I then explained to the professor why I was late and proceeded to sit in the one available desk, which was right smack in the middle of the room.

The moment I sat down, the exact same thing happened as when I was an altar boy: I had a full-blown panic attack. I sat there for forty-five minutes, clenching every muscle in my body so that no one would notice my trembling. It was so bad that I wondered if others could actually hear my heart beating. When the class ended and I walked out of the room, my feeling of relief was beyond euphoric.

After my college panic attack, again I never gave it much thought, and it didn't happen again while I was in college. Then, after I graduated, I got my first real job as a counselor in a public high school. I was twenty-two years old and a bit insecure, naturally.

About one month into my new job, the principal called me into his office and told me that he needed me to do a presentation to the staff the following Monday after school. Well, the entire week leading up to that staff meeting was pure torment. I was so nervous about having to speak in front of approximately one hundred of my colleagues that I was actually considering quitting the job. I'm not kidding! With each day that passed, and the closer I got to that upcoming Monday, my fear got worse.

When the final bell rang that Monday, I made my way to the auditorium, got up in front of all of my colleagues, and spoke for an hour. The moment I started to speak I went into a full panic attack and was scared that everyone would notice.

After my presentation ended, some of my colleagues came up to me and told me that I did a great job. I asked a couple of colleagues whom I was close with if I appeared nervous, and they all said, "Not at all." I was shocked because I couldn't understand how no one noticed the sheer terror I experienced.

Interestingly, as the years went on, I had to do more of those talks at faculty meetings, and with each one my anxiety seemed to have less of a grip on me. My subconscious came

66

to realize that it no longer needed to activate my body's alarm system because there was no actual life-threatening danger. Today I lecture all over the country in front of hundreds of people, and I don't even feel the least bit nervous. In fact, I enjoy it immensely.

Think about all of this for a moment. The simple thought of *What will people think of me?* that popped into my mind when I had to speak in front of a crowd caused so much fear and panic that I almost quit my first job. That's how strong the mind is.

I also go on live national television often, with millions of viewers watching, and sometimes I feel my body starting to go into panic mode. Thankfully I've developed a strategy that helps me slow down the anxiety. It's a strategy that I teach to many of my patients. I'll share this strategy later in the chapter.

I honestly can't tell you why I had those panic attacks when I was younger or why they still try to creep in from time to time. But I can tell you that they came from somewhere. When I was younger, I probably had a frightening experience that left a lasting imprint on my subconscious. I often wonder, if I was born thirty years later and spent most of my childhood in cyberspace, how my anxiety would have fared.

In the first chapter I talked about the increase in social anxiety that is plaguing our society, particularly in our younger citizens. The simple lack of human interaction and the reclusive lifestyle many kids have today as they scroll through social media from their bedrooms is enough to trigger substantial mental health problems, namely anxiety and depression. Couple this with all of the fear-related content they're exposed to from those handheld devices, and we've got the perfect storm—a lot of fear and anxiety. And as I mentioned earlier, the social restrictions that came during the COVID-19 pandemic made all of this worse.

A recent study published in *The Lancet* examined data sources in an attempt to quantify the mental health toll that COVID-19 restrictions had on people.[3] The authors reported a worldwide increase of more than 129 million cases of major depression and anxiety disorders compared to pre-pandemic numbers. They attributed their findings to the combined effects of the virus spread, along with stay-at-home orders, lockdowns, business closures, decreased social interaction, school closures, and more.

Unfortunately, the mental health effects were most severe for younger people, especially because the need for social interaction is stronger among young folks. But I believe there's more. During the pandemic I counseled many preteens and teens who were struggling mightily with anxiety and depression. All of them had the same thing in common. They were at home twenty-four hours a day, and because of that they spent almost all of their time online. When they weren't in their bedrooms on their phones or laptops or playing video games, their parents had the news on in the background. And pretty much all of the news was related to the pandemic, which was pretty frightening. Kids' brains absorbed all of this, whether they realized it or not.

Many of the kids and adults I counseled during that time also experienced a lot of somatic symptoms such as headaches and stomachaches. Many spent a lot of time on health websites to see what was wrong with them because they didn't realize their symptoms were stress related.

WebMD'd

Andrea was a fourteen-year-old high school freshman who was recommended to me by her pediatrician. When I met with her and her mom during our first session, I discovered Andrea had a host of physical ailments and had visited about a half dozen doctors. She often had nausea, chest pain, stomach problems, headaches, and more. She had been to the endocrinologist, neurologist, and cardiologist. Andrea thought for sure she was dying. But each doctor ruled out any illness and told her she should see a mental health professional because they believed her issue was anxiety.

Within five minutes of meeting with Andrea and her mom, I knew for sure the doctors were right. When I asked Andrea if she frequented any medical websites to research her ailments, she told me she did so almost obsessively.

I've counseled many Andreas over the years, both children and adults. These people suffer from something called somatic symptom disorder, formerly known as hypochondria, and the internet is making this condition worse. In fact, the easy availability of health information on the web makes it easier for people to develop this disorder. Although this type of medical access is helpful for people who want to make informed decisions about their health, it can be disastrous for people who tend to worry more than others.

To someone suffering with somatic symptom disorder, a simple headache can mean disaster. They visit a medical website, read about their symptoms, and believe they have a brain tumor. An upset stomach can mean cancer, and minor chest pain is sure to be a heart attack.

The human mind has a tremendous influence on the body, so much so that it can convince the body to feel something that isn't real. This is called somatization, and it often causes people to feel the symptoms they read about online, even though they don't have the condition or disease. According to Dr. Adam Kaplan, a neuroscientist at Johns Hopkins, "People are very suggestible, patients read about various ailments, they sort of hypnotize themselves into believing they have these conditions."[4]

When I was thirty-eight years old, I felt a mild pain in my chest, nothing serious, but of course I immediately went on WebMD and got myself into a tizzy. At the time, I worked out every day at the gym, didn't have an ounce of body fat, didn't eat red meat or desserts, and had a cholesterol level of 160. Yet I was still a little bit worried, considering that heart disease ran in my family.

A dad with whom I coached Little League baseball happened to be a heart surgeon at a local hospital, so I explained my situation to him. He actually laughed at me and said, "Tom, there is no way you are going to have a heart attack at thirty-eight, especially in the shape you're in." He told me that if it would make me feel better, he could recommend a cardiologist in the area. I went to the cardiologist and had all kinds of tests done, an EKG, stress test, you name it. And of course, I was fine. I vowed to never go on WebMD again.

The self-diagnosis-made-easy we get from medical websites perpetuates anxiety and can lead to hypochondriac behavior. This is just another example of how too much information, namely all of the information that's available online, can get in our heads. These are learned fears, not innate fears.

Fear Learned

I've outlined a lot in this chapter about the impressionability of our minds and how the images and information coming to us from all over the place cause legitimate fear and anxiety. But there's more.

According to a March 2021 *Fatherly* article, children are so easily scared because that's how brain development works. The article explored the causes of fear in children and whether they come from nature or nurture. The scientists in the article identified two types of fear: innate fears, which we are born with, and learned fears, which are the ones we pick up along the way.

It turns out that the vast majority of fears are learned, and there are only two basic innate fears: fear of falling and fear of loud noises. According to Dr. Seth Norrhjolm, a neurologist at Emory University,

> our brains operate along two neural pathways: the low road, which causes immediate reaction, and the high road, in which your brain assesses the situation. "The low road circuitry goes from your senses—your eyes and ears—to the amygdala, then to your muscles, adrenal glands, and spinal cord."[5]

So if you're watching a horror movie or watching dozens of fear-provoking videos on YouTube, your fight-or-flight response is activated. This "low road" reaction is the body's natural alarm system that I explained earlier. A loud thunderclap or a dish falling and breaking causes a "low road" reaction.

Norrhjolm explained that preschoolers' thinking, because it isn't fully developed yet, is very concrete and reactionary, but as they get older and learn through life experiences, the frontal cortex of the brain becomes more developed.

Let's summarize all of this for a moment. *Jaws* frightened the heck out of millions of people, including me. It's clear that the things we fear are mostly learned, meaning that they come from our experiences. We also know that children's minds are more impressionable than fully developed adult minds. And most importantly, our children are exposed to endless amounts of images and videos, many of which can trigger fear.

Many graphic videos that circulate through social media aren't even real. Some are altered to create shock value, but our brains don't realize this. The more shocking or frightening, the more likely a video is to go viral. *Jaws* isn't real. Neither is *Friday the 13th*, but certain areas of our brains lack the ability to identify what is real and what isn't; they just react. So the question is, What can we do about this when there is so much frightening content directed at our children?

Besting Fear and Panic

So far I've talked about how the brain processes images, thereby shaping our thoughts and emotions. It simply reacts naturally to everything we see and experience in life. That's what it's built to do. Wouldn't it make sense to protect our children from being exposed to negative and fear-provoking images and, instead, expose them to safer and more pleasant things? What if we could control what they experience? We can.

If you pause for a moment and think about it, the world is not a predominately bad and dangerous place. It just seems like it is because that is all we see on the news. The majority of us don't experience many actual, real-life, terrifying events. We don't get chased by grizzly bears, get carjacked, or get shot at very often, if at all. We just see these events happening to other people through our screens. Fear sells.

The truth is that the world is a wonderful, safe place. Sure, there are areas in our country with a lot of crime, and there are tragic events that happen on any given day, but it's always been that way. The difference is that these events are now captured on video and immediately transmitted to our phones and computers. This kind of technology didn't exist until recently. In the past we simply would not have known about specific crimes, kidnappings, or car crashes. Now we see it all, and so do our kids.

The question I have is this: If our children were less exposed to negative content and instead practiced the skill of positive thinking, which is not automatic, would doing so prevent fear and anxiety from setting in? Could it help to undo any anxiety and fear that already exist? Without question. Let's talk about how we can do this.

First, I want to share a strategy you can teach to your children if they currently suffer from anxiety or panic attacks. It's a strategy I personally use, the one I earlier promised I would share. I'll use myself as an example. Here's how it works. When I am about to go on television, I sometimes feel the beginning stages of a panic attack. This happens because my subconscious mind is sending me fear thoughts along the lines of, *What if you mess up?* or *What if the host asks you a question you don't know the answer to?* or *What will all of the people watching think of you?* My heart starts to race.

As soon as I recognize my heart is racing, I immediately take a healthy, deep breath of air. This does one of two things. First, taking that deep breath requires using my conscious mind. That means I'm present. I'm in the now. Consciously focusing my mind on that breath of air means I have separated myself from my wandering subconscious mind that is sending me those fear thoughts.

Next, after I have fully exhaled, I hold my breath for as long as I can. This deprives my body of oxygen, which makes my heart rate automatically begin to slow down. I then take another breath and repeat the process. Then, *bingo*, my mind registers that my heart rate has slowed down and tells me that I am now calm instead of panicked.

This is a strategy you can easily teach to children. It requires daily practice to master, but with diligence your children will learn how to redirect a panic attack and replace it with calm self-control. The key is becoming aware of the first sign of any physical symptoms and then immediately remembering to consciously focus on each breath.

We hear all the time that breathing helps with panic and anxiety, but it's not really the breaths of air warding off the panic; it's the fact that we must be conscious and present in order to take that intentional breath of air. When we are present and conscious, we tame the subconscious, which is where the fear thoughts come from.

Here's another strategy you can teach your children, one that is more preventative, designed to keep children from developing panic or anxiety. This is going to require some work on your end, and you'll get some pushback from your children, but it is well worth it.

The first thing I want you to do is grab a pen and paper.

Now, spend some time going through each child's entire day, from the moment they wake up until they go to sleep at night. What's the first thing your children do when they wake up and roll out of bed?

If they're teenagers, more than likely the first thing they do is check their phone. Write it down. What are they doing as they're eating breakfast and in the passenger seat on the way to school? They're probably staring at their phone. Write it down. What about the television? Is the news on in the background? Is the news on in the car? If so, write it down. How about when they are at school all day? Although you're not with them, you can probably envision your child walking through the hallways staring at their phone. Write it down.

Continue to write down everything you can think of that your children's brains are digesting on a daily basis. I'm sure a lot of it is fun and entertaining, but I bet a lot of it isn't. The big question is whether or not all of the images and videos they absorb all day long strengthen their minds. Would you say they are good for their mental health or not very good for their mental health? Write it down.

Once you have an inventory of where your children's minds are all day long, take a look at your list and ask yourself if all of this is healthy for their minds. You'll find that it isn't.

Next, I want you to write another list—but this time go back and imagine your own childhood. What did you do when you woke up in the morning? Write it down. What were you doing or thinking while you were eating breakfast? What were you thinking or doing while you rode your bike or bus to school or were in the passenger seat of your parents' car? Write it down. How about in the evenings? What were you doing and thinking? Write it down.

Once you have both lists, compare the two. You'll see a big difference. If your childhood was like mine, when you were a kid, you were free. You conversed with your parents at the breakfast and dinner table. You stared out the car window on the ride to school and talked to your mom or dad. You communicated face-to-face with your peers at school and out of school. You were outside more than you were inside. You were present. You were thinking. You were in control. And you likely weren't crippled by anxiety.

Now, I want you to make some changes in your household. Keep the news off when your children are around. Drastically limit the amount of time they spend hypnotized by their devices. Have face-to-face communication with your kids. Talk to them about all of this. Make them read this chapter. Get the phones out of their bedrooms. Kick your kids out the door and make them spend time outside. And, most important of all, practice what you preach by pulling yourself out of the dark hole of screen time and instead being present for your children.

CHAPTER TIPS

- Follow the rules. If a movie is rated R or a video game is rated M, don't allow your underage children to be exposed to this stuff. There's a reason they are rated as they are. Your children's brains aren't ready for it.
- Shield your children. I'm talking about keeping the news off when your children are around. I'm talking

about having any conversations about world dangers out of earshot from your children.

- If your child has developed severe anxiety to the point they don't want to go to school or don't want to be with friends, seek help. Contact a licensed mental health professional right away.

Behavior and Conduct Issues

Over the last couple of years, I've seen an incredible rise in oppositional-defiance behavior in children of all ages. Things like twelve-year-old boys calling their parents names that I cannot write on this page. I've seen countless kids have complete emotional meltdowns and throw fits just because their parents made them turn off their Xbox or took away their phones. I've even dealt with kids as young as ten becoming physically assaultive toward their parents. Something is causing this anger and emotional dysregulation, and we need to find out what it is. I'm going to explore those causes in this chapter, and I'm also going to offer some strategies you can use to help your children.

My grandfather came from Ireland at the age of nineteen with just the shirt on his back. He grew up poor and lived in a tiny thatched-roof house on a one-acre farm in County Westmeath. He and my grandmother raised my mother and her three older brothers in the Bronx. My grandfather was a tough, proud man who loved America.

My mother always had great stories about her upbringing and how honorable of a man my grandfather was. He respected others and demanded respect in return. A rule he had in his home was that if any of his children's friends came to the house, they were required to sit down with him at the kitchen table and have a conversation. That's the way it was back then. Respect your elders.

One day a teenage boy arrived at the house looking for my mother's brother Johnny. When my grandfather opened the door, he extended his hand to the boy and said, "Hello, young man." The boy ignored my grandfather's attempt at a handshake and proceeded to walk past him, exclaiming hastily, "Where's Johnny?"

As the story goes, my grandfather followed the boy into the kitchen, grabbed him by his collar and belt buckle, carried him back to the front door, and promptly tossed him out of the house. My grandfather was stocky and boasted a nineteen-inch neck. He spent his career in America working for Con Edison, building the streets of New York City with a jackhammer. He was a strong Irishman.

He was not someone to be defied. As much as I loved and respected him, I also feared him. One thing I hated most was when my grandfather was at our house for dinner, because my siblings and I weren't allowed to leave the table until every morsel of food on our plates was finished. It makes sense to me now, when I think about it, considering that my grandfather grew up so poor in Ireland and lived off the land his family owned. Every bit of food was precious.

One memory that's still etched in my mind happened when I was around eight years old. My grandfather was at our house for dinner, and although I had eaten my pork chops, the green beans I hated remained on my plate. As I got up from the dinner table, hoping that my grandfather wouldn't notice the uneaten green beans, he immediately caught on, and in his strong, Irish brogue he said, "Tommy, sit down and finish your supper."

I slumped back into my chair for what felt like an eternity and forced those green beans down my throat as my grandfather watched. No questions asked and no rebuttal. That wouldn't have been tolerated.

Although most kids today are respectful, the unprecedented amount of disrespect I see at my private practice is concerning. Chances are you've experienced some of this with one of your own children, where they say things or act in ways you never would have dared when you were a child. So, what's going on? What's changed? What happened to "Respect your elders" or "Respect your parents" or "Respect your teachers?" Let's explore.

School Defiance

According to Kalyn Belsha, a reporter for Chalkbeat, a nonprofit news organization that covers education, schools across the country have seen a recent uptick in disruptive behaviors, and experts believe it is because of the stress the pandemic has placed on children.[1] Student fights over social media posts, running out of classrooms, and trashing bathrooms have become commonplace. Alyssa Rodriguez, a Chicago social worker who was interviewed for the article, said that behavioral referrals and verbal and physical attacks were up, and that parents were worried about their children's shorter-than-usual tempers.

In Denver, Alex Magana, a principal who oversees two middle schools, also saw post-pandemic behavioral challenges as students occasionally stormed out of their classrooms and were more defiant and challenging of authority. Across the Denver school district, which serves ninety thousand students, fights were up 21 percent compared to pre-pandemic statistics.

A high school junior from Houston named Chanyce Johnson was also interviewed for the article. He believed that because students were out of school for so long, they'd forgotten how to socialize. He said that during group projects in class, for example, teachers had to urge students to talk with one another because they seemed to have forgotten how to initiate conversation. He, too, noticed more student fights than in previous years.

Another story published in the *South Florida Sun Sentinel* newspaper explored the amount of violence and behavioral issues occurring in Florida schools. Students and staff were scared every day because of the amount of student fights and assaults on teachers.[2] Reports of fights, criminal batteries, and fear of violence were happening at every school, particularly in South Florida. Some of these fights were recorded by students and posted on TikTok.

Monarch High School in Coconut Creek, Florida, saw at least ten assaults occur between September and November 2021, with several arrests made. In Palm Beach County there were sixty-eight incidents of battery and twenty-nine arrests in the same time period, while Broward County had the most incidents in that time period with 712 fights and 223 physical attacks reported.[3]

Although most of these behavioral issues were coming from teenagers, the article also reported behavioral concerns in younger children, including pre-K and kindergarten students coming to school angry and frustrated. One particularly troubled ten-year-old hit a teacher over the head with a snow globe.

Oppositional Defiance

Children and teens who exhibit these types of aggressive and defiant behaviors often suffer from a behavioral disorder known as oppositional defiant disorder (ODD). These behaviors typically take place in school and at home. ODD is mostly diagnosed in childhood. Children with ODD are often defiant, uncooperative, and hostile toward peers, parents, teachers, and other authority figures. According to Johns Hopkins Medicine, there are two main theories for why this occurs: developmental theory and learning theory.[4]

- **Developmental theory:** according to this theory, ODD starts when children are toddlers. It suggests they have trouble learning to become independent from a parent to whom they were emotionally attached, causing normal developmental issues to last beyond the toddler years.
- **Learning theory:** this theory suggests that the negative symptoms of ODD are learned because they

mirror the effects of negative reinforcement methods used by parents. Negative reinforcement allows the child to get what they want: attention and reaction from parents or other authority figures.

ODD is also more common in boys than in girls. Although young children around the age of two or three normally tend to push the boundaries by disobeying, arguing, or defying their parents, when it continues regularly into the teen years, the teen may have ODD. Oppositional defiant behavior interferes with learning and relationships with others. Here are some of the symptoms of ODD:

- Arguing with adults
- Frequent temper tantrums
- Defying rules and chores
- Constantly questioning the rules and refusing to follow them
- Purposefully annoying parents and others
- Frequent anger
- Easily annoyed by others
- Vindictiveness and revenge
- Speaking harshly or unkindly
- Hostility

Hostility in the Home

One patient of mine, John, was having a particularly difficult time managing his emotions, and his parents were at their wits' end. When I first started working with John, he was a fifteen-year-old high school freshman. His parents originally called me to see if I knew of any wilderness programs where they could send him because the fighting and arguing were out of control. His grades had also declined.

John's parents were helpless and didn't know what to do. Whenever they tried to talk to him, even in a calm manner, he would explode. After gathering all of the information, I told the parents that sending him away to a wilderness program was premature and would likely backfire. I encouraged them to bring him to me first and give it some time.

When John came to my office for his first session, he seemed relieved to have someone neutral to talk to. He felt that no one in his family listened to him and just dismissed everything he felt and everything he said. He also believed that his younger sister got away with everything and was never held accountable, but if he did the slightest thing wrong he would get punished. He felt that his parents were unjust. I connected quickly with John, and we developed a strong rapport right away, which is probably the most important part of my job.

The following week I held a family session to get a better idea of what was happening. As John's parents and sister spoke about the issues in the family, it became immediately evident that John felt he was being attacked, even though he wasn't. He became extremely defensive, verbally aggressive, and tearful. He even cursed out his parents and sister. His reaction was completely irrational. With about fifteen minutes left in the session, I asked John's parents and his sister to wait in the waiting area. I spoke alone with John for the remainder of the session.

John and I continued to meet each week, and I quickly had my finger on the problem: John was unable to control his emotions. His aggressive reaction to every little thing in his household was the root of the problem. It would also become the solution. I helped John understand that if he could change how he reacted to his parents and sister, and not get so defensive and argumentative at every little thing, then the entire temperament in the household would change.

I told John that although his family looked at him as the problem, he was actually the solution. All he needed to do was practice pausing for a couple of seconds to monitor his emotions so that he could actually think first instead of just immediately reacting with emotion.

John liked that. He took my advice and practiced hard. Gradually, John was able to change how he responded toward his family members. If any of them said something he didn't like, he would pause, breathe, and think. This allowed him to assess his emotions and keep them in check. As a result, he became far less stressed and started to excel in school again. He became a changed person, and as a result the whole family changed for the better.

The question is, Why did John become so angry, defiant, and vindictive? One thing I know for sure is that my grandfather would never have tolerated any of that behavior, nor would my own parents—but then again, that was a completely different generation. The world was different then. Oppositional and defiant behavior seems to be happening all over society, not just at school and at home.

Public Unruliness

In July 2021, the town of Avalon, New Jersey, a wealthy shore town with a median home price of $2.6 million, had to close its boardwalk and beaches. Avalon mayor Martin Pagliughi cited "unsafe and disruptive behavior" by juveniles congregating on the beaches and boardwalks who were regularly vandalizing public property, fighting, and leaving behind excessive litter.[5]

Pagliughi said that parents needed to take an active approach in managing the activities and whereabouts of their juveniles and hold them accountable for violating rules. He also blamed state juvenile justice reform for the unprecedented increase in disorderly juveniles, because the laws prohibited police from being able to do anything other than issue warnings to minors for these behaviors, even when alcohol and marijuana were involved.

Kids aren't the only members of society who are emotionally revved up; many adults are too. Rowdy and aggressive behavior has been occurring on airplanes and in retail stores throughout the country, the likes of which we've never seen before, and it is documented all over social media for our children to see. From January to July 2021 there were 2,500 reports of unruly behavior on airplanes, and 44 percent of McDonald's workers reported being physically or verbally assaulted over mask mandates.[6] One Starbucks barista said that even after mask mandates were lifted, she experienced a handful of berating, abusing customers on a daily basis.

One TikTok video that went viral showed a woman duct-taped to her seat on an American Airlines flight after she attacked flight attendants and attempted to open the plane's front door. She began biting, spitting, and attacking the attendants, which prompted the crew to restrain her.

Such aggression and unruliness have gotten so bad that, by the end of 2021, the number of reports of unruly passengers on planes rose to nearly six thousand. As a result, Delta Airlines asked the Department of Justice to place passengers convicted of unruly behavior on a no-fly list.[7]

Let's explore this rise in hostile behavior a bit more to see if we can put our finger on the problem. As I mentioned earlier, the mind is impressionable, so much so that a simple two-hour movie like *Jaws* can cause real fear and anxiety in our thoughts. Could the same be true for why we're seeing so many more kids struggling with oppositional defiant behavior? Maybe they've learned these behaviors somewhere.

Think about it. What kind of lyrics do kids listen to? How about the stuff they see on television and social media? Wouldn't you say there's a constant exposure to violence and aggression flooding their brain waves? I think the problem is a combination of everything they are exposed to on a daily basis coupled with the fact that kids spend less time socializing in person, which is how they develop social skills and emotional regulation.

Communication Breakdown

In chapter 2, I discussed the importance of social-emotional skills and how these skills are developed through in-person peer-to-peer communication. I also talked about silent alone time, which is the dialogue we have with our inner self, and the positive impact it has on self-esteem. Our children should be immersed in face-to-face interaction and silent time on a regular basis, but they aren't.

Instead, most of the communication and interaction our kids experience takes place on the screens they stare at, which usually includes a lot of unhealthy and inappropriate content. This shapes their thoughts, beliefs, and actions. Remember the students who recorded fights in their school and shared them on TikTok? Thousands of kids watched those fights and more. Over time, regular exposure to those types of violent and aggressive acts desensitizes the brain to violence. Gradually the brain processes it as "normal."

Social media is a platform where videos of school fights and other aggressive acts are shared constantly and is a place where our children spend a good chunk of their waking hours. Social media is also where unhappy, frustrated people can take out their dissatisfaction in the form of tweets and other posts. If you have Facebook, for example, spend some time scrolling through other people's posts and see for yourself the way some of them treat each other and how they respond to someone who disagrees with them. It can get nasty.

In addition to all of this, every mainstream news story now funnels through social media, and most of these stories are all doom, gloom, and fear. They're designed to agitate people, and they do a good job of it. I refer to social media as the tailpipe of mainstream media. Not too many happy stories there. Have you ever thought about the impact countless hours of this stuff has on your children's thoughts and emotions?

Social media has become my psychology laboratory. Although I don't post very often on social media, I do spend some time studying human behavior. I'm often shocked by the posts, comments, and reactions coming from grown adults. It's like the world has taken an anger pill. If you are seeing these things on your own social media platforms, you better believe your children are too.

So far we've talked a little bit about what might be causing all of these troubling behavioral issues—less social interaction and the constant exposure to hostile and violent content online. However, there's another piece to this puzzle, something we adults didn't get nearly as much of as our own children do: instant gratification. Many of today's kids get pretty much whatever they want, when they want it. It is all just a click away. And if they don't get what they want? Well, you know what can happen.

Instant Gratification

My parents were married at nineteen, right before my dad was sent off to Vietnam to fight for the country. My oldest sister was born nine months later, and by the time my parents were twenty-five they had three more children, my brother and my twin sister and me. And they were flat broke.

My dad struggled to make ends meet and worked as many side jobs as he could after work and on weekends to put food on the table, while my mom juggled a five-year-old, a three-year-old, and two infant twins. Needless to say, my parents didn't have the resources to get my siblings and me all of the things we wanted, and that turned out to be a good thing.

I fell in love with baseball when I was around three years old, and I was pretty good at it. When my older brother started Little League, I would stand behind the home plate fence, eagerly waiting for my chance to get on that field. Two years later my chance came, but there was one problem. I didn't have a baseball glove.

Fortunately, my uncle gave me his old, worn-out glove from when he was a kid. The glove was crusty, moldy, and smelly because it had been left out in the rain too many times, but I was happy to have it. Somehow we brought that glove back from its rigor mortis, and I used it for several years. I did not ask my parents for a new one, because I knew they couldn't afford it. I waited until Christmas for a new one.

In the fourth grade I also took up basketball, and again I had a problem as I didn't have a basketball to practice with. My uncle came through again and gave me his old ball. The ball was pretty bald, which meant it had no grip to it, and it didn't hold air very well. But it didn't matter because it was mine, and that meant I could practice at the local park down the street. Again, I didn't ask my parents if they could buy me a better basketball, because I knew they couldn't, so I waited until my birthday to get a new one.

I share this because when I was growing up families didn't have the same resources that many families today have. Parents couldn't just go out and buy their kids things just because they wanted them, and wanted them now. We had to wait, and that helped us understand the value of things and the importance of delayed gratification.

Today, our kids don't experience much delayed gratification. If they need a new basketball, baseball bat, or phone, we get it for them. Not much waiting. Just go to Amazon and there it is on the doorstep the next day. Need an answer to a question? Just Google it and there's your answer, immediately. No research, no thinking, no elbow grease. Want to watch the latest movie that just came out? Boom! Click a button on your television remote and there you have it. No driving over to Blockbuster Video and hoping that it's available. Hungry for some Burger King? Bam! A DoorDash driver will deliver it right to your front door.

Our kids have grown up in a world of instant gratification. Virtually anything they want or need comes to them instantaneously, requiring very little effort to obtain. I hate to use the word *spoiled*, but that's how a lot of children are raised today. This can lead to entitlement, which means they believe they deserve what they want, when they want it, and if they don't get it they throw a fit. Have you experienced this with your children? If you haven't, then you are definitely doing something right.

I was recently speaking to a woman I know about her son. She was concerned that he had become a bit too attached to a particular friend and wasn't branching out and meeting other kids. Her son's friend was at her house all the time, and apparently didn't have much structure in his own home. There weren't many rules or chores and he was a bit entitled.

The woman told me that her son and this boy were playing a video game together at her house when she heard a loud bang come from the basement. Apparently the friend had gotten killed in the game and became so enraged that he threw his brand-new iPhone against the wall and broke it. The boy's father immediately bought him a new one. There were no consequences for his behavior.

Think about this for a moment. The boy threw his phone against the wall, broke it, and the next day a new one was waiting for him. This is a textbook example of a child who is instantly gratified and entitled. He's also an example of a child who clearly gets "high" on video games a lot, and just like any other drug, when the high wears off, withdrawal sets in—hence throwing his phone against the wall.

Chasing Dopamine

A recent essay by Dr. Anna Lembke that appeared in the *Wall Street Journal* explores how many people in America and other wealthy countries are getting hooked on dopamine, the neurotransmitter associated with pleasure and reward.[8] During her career as a psychiatrist, she has seen more and more patients suffering from anxiety, depression, and aggression, including healthy young people who come from stable, loving families. She says that it's not because of trauma, social dislocation, or poverty but from too much dopamine. Whenever our children do something they enjoy, like playing video games or combing through their social media feeds, their brain releases a little bit of dopamine, making them feel good and instantly gratifying them.

One of the most important discoveries in the field of neuroscience that Dr. Lembke explained is that both pleasure and pain are processed by the same part of the brain. The brain tries hard to keep them balanced, but whenever either pain or pleasure tips in one direction, it is hard for the brain to restore the balance, which is known as homeostasis. In other words, as soon as dopamine is released, the brain adapts to it by reducing the number of dopamine receptors that are stimulated. This causes the brain to level out by tipping to the side of pain, which is why pleasure is usually followed by feeling hungover. This then leads to a natural tendency to counteract the pain by going back to the source of pleasure for another dose.

Lembke's essay also explores how the brain evolved this fine-tuned balance over millions of years, when pleasures were scarce and dangers were all around. In our modern

93

world, we have an overwhelming abundance of addictive substances, from sugar to drugs to, of course, electronics. We now have texting, web surfing, tweeting, online gaming, and shopping, all of which are engineered to be addictive. Those flashing lights and sounds, and all of those alerts, "likes," and "streaks" provide the brain with a constant dopamine drip, just a click away. Talk about instant gratification.

The moment we stop, we experience universal symptoms of withdrawal, such as irritability, anxiety, insomnia, and more. We crave more. Perhaps the most eye-opening thought I took from Lembke's essay is that despite having all of these pleasurable things around us, and access to just about anything we want, as a whole we're more miserable than ever.

The rates of suicide, anxiety, depression, and physical pain have increased all over the world. The wealthier the country, the higher the rate of these problems. Americans reported being less happy in 2018 than in 2008, despite having access to so much more.

Lembke asks her patients to give up their digital drug of choice for a month, which is long enough to give the brain time to reset its dopamine balance. I challenge my patients to do the same with their children. This certainly isn't easy, considering the pain their children will experience from withdrawal and the oppositional-defiant behavior that often comes with it, but in the long term it is worth it.

I have so many stories of kids who are so addicted to either video games or some other screen device that they withdraw really hard when their parents tell then to turn it off or take it away. Larry is one example. His mom called me in the fall of 2021 to schedule an appointment. Larry was twelve years old and was disrespectful, defiant, and mean to his parents.

When I met them the first time, his parents said that it was nearly impossible to get him to do his homework. It would turn into an argument every day, causing Larry to become vindictive and nasty. His behavior was affecting everyone in the family.

Larry was also getting into some trouble at school. He had been thrown out of class and sent to the principal's office several times in the two weeks prior to our first session because he was disrupting the class and disrespecting his teachers.

I asked a lot of questions during our meeting and concluded that Larry was fully addicted to his smartphone. All he wanted to do was be on it, and nothing else mattered to him. All of his opposition and defiance were related to using his phone. In other words, whenever he was told to do his homework it meant he would not have access to the phone that provided him with a constant stream of dopamine, which he craved without really understanding why.

Anytime Larry wasn't allowed to have his smartphone, it caused withdrawal, much like a drug addict who runs out of drugs. Homework certainly wasn't giving him his fix of dopamine the way his phone was, nor was being at school in a classroom where he couldn't use his phone and chase that dopamine rush. I explained all of this to Larry and his parents and challenged Larry to a smartphone fast. Thankfully they listened, and Larry's behavior gradually improved.

Opposition, defiance, violence, and other behavioral issues are more common in recent years than in previous generations. There's just too much stimulation and too much dopamine and, as a result, too much crashing. And because there's so much exposure to violence and hostility there is too little exposure to kindness and goodness.

God Canceled

As our society continues to move further away from a faith in a higher power, a power that embodies all that is good, the doors become open for all that is bad. The attempt to remove God from our society isn't new. It's been happening for a while now. I believe this is partly why there's so much more violence, crime, hopelessness, and defiance in our society. Think about it. What is badness? It's the absence of good, the same way that darkness is the absence of light. God represents all that is good, and when God is removed darkness takes over. That's how I look at it.

George Barna, a professor at Arizona Christian University, wrote a sixty-two-page research report intended to obtain insights into the Millennial generation, those born between 1984 through 2002. According to Barna, "When we replace God with people—or nothing—we become moral free agents with no higher calling, no slate of moral imperatives or guidelines, and no eternal consequences for our temporal choices."[9]

In the 1940s and '50s nearly 90 percent of Americans claimed they believed in God, while barely a third of millennials today do. "By 'canceling' God, we seek to empower ourselves and replace His authority with our own through feelings, human rationale, or expedience as viable justifications for unbiblical choices. By denying His existence we alleviate any personal responsibility to a Creator for our actions," says Barna.

Something else Barna discovered was that Millennials in his survey didn't have as much respect for human beings as adults from previous generations. Millennials were 15 percentage points less likely than Gen Xers to say they treat others the way they want to be treated and twice as likely to say they respect those who hold the same religious or political views.

Although Millennials are well known for their advocacy toward tolerance, they emerged from Barna's survey as the least tolerant generation, by their own admission, of people who hold different views from their own. Furthermore, they were 28 percentage points more likely than Baby Boomers to admit they are "committed to getting even" with those who wrong them.[10]

Millennials also indicated they had less respect for life in general. For example, they were half as likely as other adults to say that life is sacred and twice as likely as older adults to diminish the value of human life by describing human beings as either "material substance only" or their very existence as "an illusion."

Some of Barna's other key findings are as follows:

- 29 percent of younger Millennials (ages 18–25) have some type of mental disorder.
- 54 percent of those surveyed acknowledged some degree of emotional fragility or even mental illness.
- 96 percent of Millennials lack a biblical worldview.
- 75 percent reported that they lack meaning and purpose in life.
- Only one-third claimed to believe in God.[11]

Hope Is a Good Thing

Fortunately there is hope, because today's children are no different from previous generations; only the world around

97

them has altered. How do we raise our children to be mentally and emotionally strong in a world that's filled with so much destruction and so many challenges? We have to keep our children out of that world as best we can and build a better world for them, one we want for them. A world founded on love, guidance, and respect. A world where we have deep, meaningful conversations with our children all the time and protect them as best we can from the bad things going on around them and from all of the temptations dangled in front of them. By no means is this easy, but then again parenting is not meant to be easy. Some hard-nosed parenting will be necessary.

The best way to protect your child from being sucked into the negatives that surround them starts with the word *no*, a word that must be used a lot. Will they fuss and complain when your rules differ from their peers' rules? Most certainly. But we can no longer just conform to the way the majority lives. We can't allow our kids to simply fall in line as we cross our fingers and hope our children don't get lost in cyberspace.

Instead, we must talk to our children, and talk to them a lot, about what is right and what is moral. They will challenge us and manipulate us, and that's ok. Because in the end, if we provide our children with love, discipline, and accountability, they will thank us later. The end result will be young adults filled with confidence, grace, and strength, not hostility, defiance, and anger. What more can we ask for?

If your child is already exhibiting oppositional and defiant behaviors and you think it's too late to undo what has been done, you're wrong. It's never too late. It will require you to step up to the plate, put aside any anger, guilt, or fear, and take action. You will need to do an about-face, lay down the law, and stick to it. If this means taking away your child's phone or gaming system, then that's what you need to do. If it means taking your teenager's car away, then that's what you must do. It will feel like a setback because your child's behavior will likely get worse before it gets better, but it will be worth it in the end. They will learn that their behavior isn't tolerated and that there are consequences in life. We call this tough love, and it is a necessary part of the parenting handbook.

CHAPTER TIPS

- Slow the dopamine drip. Just because children have easy access to just about everything they want, providing them with all of it will backfire. Teach your children delayed gratification.
- Keep your children away from violent content. The more the brain is exposed to violent and inappropriate content, the more it becomes normal to the brain.
- Teach your children to treat you the way they treat their friends' parents. Most kids who are defiant and disrespectful toward their parents are usually polite and respectful to other adults. Wouldn't it make sense for them to also be polite to the adults closest to them, the ones who do everything for them, their parents?

- Learn to say no. I've always said that the most important word in the parental vocabulary should be the word *no*. When we say yes to everything, our children can become entitled and spoiled, which inevitably leads to defiant behavior.

Substance Abuse

T he first school I worked for when I was a rookie school counselor in 1995 was a special education vocational high school that served approximately two hundred emotionally disturbed students. One of my roles was to provide weekly group counseling for students who were in violation of the school's substance abuse policy. The policy stated that if a student was suspected of being under the influence of drugs or alcohol, state law required the school to send the student for a drug and alcohol urine test. Those who tested positive were required to be assessed by an approved substance abuse treatment facility and were also required to meet with me for in-school counseling.

One of my first counseling groups included four freshman boys, all of whom were caught smoking marijuana in the back of the school. The format of the group was psychoeducational, meaning that we focused more on decision-making and the dangers and consequences of substance abuse. All four boys willingly came each week and genuinely looked forward to it. It was a great experience for them and for me.

Unfortunately, one of the boys, Kevin, didn't take my advice during our group meetings and eventually became a crack cocaine addict at the age of fifteen. I worked with his parents to find a higher level of care, and he spent the next several years in and out of rehab. Several years after he graduated high school, I ran into him at a local supermarket where he was working. He had no front teeth and told me he'd been sober for a year. I'm not sure what happened to Kevin, but nearly thirty years later I still think about him.

After I left the vocational school and accepted a similar position at another high school, the majority of students' substance abuse violations were still marijuana related. I saw my fair share of students who were abusing or addicted to more potent drugs like cocaine, but it certainly wasn't the norm.

Around 2008, things began to change fast. Teenagers across America were beginning to experiment with prescription drugs, namely Oxycontin, including a group of kids at my school. Oxy is a powerful prescription narcotic often referred to as "rich man's heroin." The kids in my school who were experimenting with it would chop up the white pill with a razor blade and snort it.

Most of them came from stable families, but because they were teenagers they were naïve and didn't know what they were getting themselves into. They didn't understand the serious consequences of experimenting with Oxycontin. They

102

didn't know it was one of the most addictive substances on earth, similar to heroin.

When a person gets addicted to Oxy, which can happen very quickly, it becomes unaffordable, especially for teenagers. Back then a single 60 milligram pill of Oxycontin sold for around $60 on the black market, while an entire bundle of heroin, which is ten bags, went for around the same price. Once a person becomes addicted to Oxy they often transition to heroin because they can get ten times the amount for the same price. And because heroin has become so much purer over the years, they don't need to inject it intravenously to get high; they can snort it.

Several of my students became heroin addicts. It was a lot of work on my end, dealing with parents and school administration and helping these kids find the right rehabilitation facilities. Sadly, several died from overdoses within a few years of graduating high school, as did many more in neighboring towns and throughout the country.

Experimentation to Addiction

When I opened my private counseling practice in 2001, one of my first patients was a sixteen-year-old, Brian, who was referred to me by one of the counselors at his school because he was in violation of the school's substance abuse policy for marijuana use. Brian was a handsome, athletic kid who came from a good family, but like many teenagers he was a know-it-all.

Brian saw absolutely no problem with marijuana and candidly told me that he had the right to try every drug possible and planned to do so. He wasn't disrespectful toward me, he just felt strongly about his beliefs. This know-it-all mentality is very common among teenagers, as you probably know if you have one. Eventually I was able to get through to Brian, and he stopped smoking marijuana. But after three months, he saw no use in quitting and started smoking it again.

Eventually Brian began to experiment with other drugs like LSD and cocaine. At that point I referred him to a higher level of care, an outpatient substance abuse treatment facility in the area. He enrolled in their intensive outpatient program, also known as an IOP. IOPs are three-hour group counseling sessions where participants meet three to four times a week after school. They receive weekly drug tests and are expected to follow the rules. If they fail the drug tests and don't take the program seriously, they're then referred to an even higher level of care known as inpatient treatment. Inpatient programs are typically twenty-eight-day programs where patients live at the facility and receive many hours of therapy per day. Brian eventually ended up in an inpatient program because he became addicted to heroin.

As the years passed, I kept in touch with Brian's father. He would call me almost every week for advice. I felt bad for him because he loved his son so much but had no control over him. Brian eventually got clean and had a good senior year in high school. He was accepted to the University of Arizona, where he attended.

During his first semester in college, he unfortunately relapsed on heroin and did something very stupid and impulsive. He got access to a gun and robbed a bank. That's the type of thing heroin can make a person do, because it's so addictive, and addicts will often do anything to get it. Brian was caught and sentenced to ten years in prison. The federal prison he was placed in had a program for drug addicts that was hard to get into because of limited space. By the grace of God Brian got into the program, made incredible progress, and was released early on parole.

Having a child who is addicted to drugs or alcohol is one of the most challenging and devastating things a parent can go through. Schools do everything they can to steer kids away from gateway drugs like nicotine, alcohol, and marijuana. Everything from Scared Straight to DARE to lecturers to countless other programs have been implemented by schools in an effort to promote drug awareness and prevention.

Parents start the conversation with their children when they're young and continue to preach to them about the dangers of addictive substances, yet kids still experiment with them. Marijuana, for example, is a gateway drug, meaning that it can lead to harder and heavier drugs like cocaine and heroin.

I've never met a cocaine or heroin addict who didn't start first with marijuana or alcohol. Find me one person whose first drug experience was cocaine or heroin, not marijuana or alcohol. You won't be able to. Even though everyone knows that marijuana use can lead to using more powerful drugs, somehow it has become legal in many states.

Marijuana Legalization

If in 2007 I had grabbed ten random teenagers off the street and asked them what their thoughts were about marijuana, nine out of ten would have said that it's no good. If I were to grab ten teenagers today and ask them the same question, nine out of ten would say that marijuana is no big deal. What's changed?

105

If you think back to a little over a decade ago, marijuana smokers were a sort of secret society, unless of course you attended a Grateful Dead concert. People who smoked marijuana didn't advertise it to everyone, and it wasn't something you'd hear celebrities or other public figures talk about too much.

Then that changed. Influential and famous people began talking openly about their own marijuana use. This continued for years, and eventually marijuana smoking became a kind of normal part of society. Rappers, politicians, athletes, and actors began glorifying it and even promoting it. You'd hear it in their songs, see it in movies, and so forth. A universal consciousness followed, and marijuana smoking became a harmless, cool thing to do. It became trendy.

Soon thereafter, state politicians began legalizing it. They figured that if the majority of people had no problem with it, then they could pass legislation and make it legal. They saw dollar signs and their eyes lit up. Legalization meant tax revenue, and so the cycle of marijuana acceptance grew. Unfortunately, the message also seeped into the minds of vulnerable kids. More kids began using it. Why wouldn't they? After all, if it is legal it must not be that dangerous, right?

Clearly, I'm not an advocate of marijuana or marijuana legalization, and that is because I see exactly what it does to the teenagers I counsel every day. If an adult uses marijuana for medical purposes, so be it; that's their choice, and I won't question that. But kids using it? That is an entirely different story.

I mentioned earlier that teenagers by nature are know-it-alls. The reason is because they don't have fully developed brains yet. The frontal lobe of the brain, the part responsible for impulsivity, decision-making, and risky behavior, doesn't fully develop until around age twenty-five. That's why kids do so many stupid things like driving ninety miles per hour down the highway, jumping off thirty-foot cliffs into small pools of water, or chugging shot after shot of whiskey at a party. You don't see too many fifty-year-olds doing those things.

Here's how marijuana starts as experimentation and then leads to bigger problems. Let's say you have a fourteen-year-old freshman. He had good grades in middle school, played plenty of sports, and never had any problems. He then gets to high school, meets a new group of kids, and begins going to the park with them every day after school to play basketball. One day one of his new friends whips out a joint or a vape pen and smokes some weed. Your son is a bit shocked but doesn't say anything. He continues going to the park with his new friends and gradually, one by one, everyone in his friend group is partaking in the marijuana smoking.

Even though you've told your son since he was a toddler to stay away from marijuana, and he understood, he now feels a lot of peer pressure and decides to roll the dice. He smokes marijuana for the first time with his friends and experiences a feeling he has never had before—and he didn't drop dead. It wasn't as dangerous and scary as he thought. In fact, it felt great. Maybe everything that celebrities and social media influencers said about marijuana being cool and harmless was right and you, his parents, were wrong.

The first marking period of freshman year ends, and although your son's grades are ok, not great, you suspect something is going on. You search his room and are shocked when you open his underwear drawer and find a bunch of vape pens, cartridges, and other drug paraphernalia. You and your spouse immediately sit your son down and interrogate him. He tells you that he's holding it for a friend and that he has only tried it once (even though he's been using it daily for several months). You give him the benefit of the doubt and keep a close eye on him for a while.

Everything seems fine, until you get his next report card. He's failing two classes and has a D in another. He's also lost all interest in sports and his family, and he only wants to be with his friends. Gradually things get worse. You find more paraphernalia, and before you know it you're calling a counselor for an appointment.

This is a textbook example of what marijuana does to many kids. Once they get involved in it, it often takes over their lives. They lose interest in things, stop playing sports, and stop participating in activities they used to love. Marijuana strips kids of their motivation and potential because when they smoke it they don't want to do much of anything, especially schoolwork. They just want to get high.

This often sets in motion a vicious cycle, because the more involved they get with marijuana, the more the important things in their lives begin to crumble around them. They fall behind in school, there's constant tension in the home, and they become very stressed because somewhere in the back of their brain they know they're going nowhere fast.

But rather than recognizing this and doing something about it like quitting marijuana, they feel overwhelmed and stressed. So instead of taking on the stress and getting back on track, what do they do? They keep smoking more marijuana, because the moment they do so all stress is relieved. This becomes a terrible cycle of self-medicating that they can't seem to get out of. And the longer it goes on, the further behind they get, the worse the stress gets, and the more they smoke to avoid dealing with that stress.

Nothing I'm talking about here is new. Kids have been smoking marijuana for decades—but what has changed is the THC levels in the marijuana kids smoke today. It is substantially higher than it was just ten years ago. THC is the main ingredient in marijuana that causes a person to feel high. In the 1990s the average amount of THC in marijuana was less than 4 percent. By 2014 it averaged around 14 percent.[1] Today's concentrated marijuana products can contain as much as 90 percent THC.

This is particularly troublesome for young people because crucial brain development is still occurring. The younger a person begins using drugs, including marijuana, the more it impacts healthy brain development and the more likely they are to become drug addicted. It's also the reason why we're seeing more hospital emergency room visits for marijuana-induced psychotic episodes. Recently, for the first time in my twenty-five-year career, I witnessed this at my private practice.

Marijuana's Psychological and Physical Effects

A former patient of mine was a marijuana fanatic. He couldn't get enough of it. When he was fifteen years old, I began seeing him for counseling because he had developed anxiety. At that time he was an excellent student and athlete but loved marijuana more. He didn't want to believe me every time I told him that his anxiety was caused by the marijuana, and that using marijuana wasn't the solution to ameliorating it.

By the time he was a senior in high school, his marijuana smoking had gotten so bad that he was high 24/7. His parents sent him to rehab, much to his reluctance, but as soon as he came out of rehab he began using again.

Against my professional advice, his parents sent him away to college, and within two weeks he was arrested and thrown out of the college for selling marijuana. He gradually found his way back to my office because I was the only one he trusted, and that's when something strange began to happen.

He became psychotic. He believed people were following him. He thought the FBI was tracking him, and he got into verbal altercations with roommates and neighbors because he believed they were all out to get him. He was so addicted to marijuana that he refused to believe his psychotic episodes had anything to do with his marijuana use.

Although I have counseled many teens and young adults who have experienced severe psychological problems from smoking marijuana, I've also seen physical reactions to marijuana. One of them is a new, disturbing health trend known as "cannabinoid hyperemesis syndrome" (CHS), also called "scromiting."

Teens who suffer from this marijuana-induced condition have episodes of violent vomiting that are so painful they scream while they are vomiting. It can occur when teenagers use marijuana regularly for a long period of time and often happens because of the high levels of THC.

According to Newport Academy, a teen residential treatment facility,

> the availability of cannabis gummy edibles makes it easy for teens to ingest extreme amounts of THC. Cannabis gummy edibles take longer to act, which means teens may consume more of them, and the THC also stays in the system longer.

Weekly or more frequent vaping and smoking can also cause scromiting episodes.[2]

Approximately one-third of those who smoke marijuana at least twenty days a month suffer from scromiting. Additionally, just about every teenager who develops the condition uses marijuana at least once a week and about two-thirds of them have been using it for more than a year. Newport Academy's website provides excellent research on the long-term effects of chronic teen marijuana use. Here are some highlights:

- Consuming cannabis with THC levels over 10 percent increases the likelihood of a marijuana-related psychotic episode.
- Teen marijuana use can have damaging effects on brain development.
- Marijuana use in adolescents is associated with increase in suicidal thoughts and attempts.
- Those who use marijuana prior to age twelve are more likely to develop anxiety, depression, and schizophrenia.
- Adults who began smoking marijuana as teenagers lost an average of eight IQ points.
- Students who use marijuana are more likely to do poorly in school and drop out.[3]

If you suspect your teenager is using marijuana, here are some signs to look out for:

- Red eyes
- Fatigue

- Forgetfulness
- Increased appetite outside of usual mealtimes
- Silliness and acting out of character
- Talking loudly
- Irritability
- Loss of interest in activities that were previously enjoyable
- Hanging out with a new friend group
- Difficulty concentrating
- Stealing from family members

The Lost Boys

A twenty-one-year-old young man recently came to me for his first appointment, and I could instantly feel his depression. I knew he was a marijuana user. I started with some small talk and asked him if he worked or was in school. He responded, "I do nothing." He didn't attend college or have a job. All he did was sleep, smoke weed, and play video games.

I then asked him to rate his overall level of happiness on a scale of one to ten, ten being the highest. His was a three. I asked if he thought marijuana had anything to do with his depression, and he exclaimed, "Absolutely not! It helps me."

Professionally, I knew that if he quit smoking marijuana he'd eventually see substantial improvement in his motivation and happiness, but I also knew that he was in deep denial and there was no way I could pull out a magic wand and get him to quit smoking marijuana in just one session.

Over the last five years, I've seen an unbelievable uptick in young men like the one I just mentioned. Just about every week I get phone calls from anxious parents who are desperate to get help for their young adult sons. Some of them fail out of college after the first semester because they can't handle it. Others barely work and sleep until 2:00 p.m. every day in their childhood beds. Still others are overwhelmed with anxiety, never really leave the house, and have no plans for adulting. All are chronic marijuana smokers. I call them the lost boys.

The parents of these lost boys seem helpless and confused, and they fear their sons won't amount to anything in life. Unfortunately, many of these parents are right. So what is going on?

In every one of these cases, these young men began using marijuana as teenagers and progressed with their use, meaning that eventually they weren't just smoking marijuana for fun on the weekends but on a daily basis, sometimes all day long. As a result they lost all direction in life. They lost any form of motivation and passion, and as the clock ticked they became more and more anxious about their futures.

In most cases they're in total denial that marijuana has anything to do with their lack of direction, initiative, or motivation. Instead they avoid all fears of failure by lighting up and getting high. Doing so numbs their mind from thoughts of failure, essentially self-medicating them from these realities. The solution is to stop smoking marijuana and face the anxiety and thoughts of failure head-on. This isn't easy, but it's the only way out.

Stephen was an eighteen-year-old college freshman who came to me for help. He lived in New Jersey and had recently completed his first semester at a college in North Carolina.

113

It was a terrible experience for him. He hated the school and hated living in the dorm. He stopped attending classes after the first couple of weeks and just stayed by himself in the dorm smoking marijuana all day.

By the time he came to me for counseling, he was completely depressed and had no idea what he was going to do. I was able to get him to agree to stop smoking marijuana and enroll at a local community college the following semester.

During our weekly sessions, I pushed him to challenge himself, and he did. He had a goal of doing well at the community college and then applying as a transfer student to a school in South Carolina. It was a lofty goal for him, because it meant that for the first time in his life he was going to have to try hard academically in order to do well enough to be admitted to the school.

He did just that. He finished the semester at the community college with a 3.9 GPA, applied to the school in South Carolina, and was accepted. More importantly, Stephen lifted himself from his depressed funk and his self-medicating marijuana use. He became supermotivated and confident. Stephen had been on the brink of being a lost boy, but he found his way.

Folks, the stories like the ones I presented are preventable. It requires work on our end. We have to constantly watch our kids while they're young and in their teen years. We must have zero tolerance when it comes to drug use, including marijuana. Kids like Stephen, and the others I mentioned, unintentionally fell down a deep, dark hole simply because they didn't know any better.

When we have conversations with our teens about the dangers of drugs and alcohol, they may roll their eyes and think we're overreacting, but we have to remember that they're our children and we're the parents. We are in charge, and we simply know better than they do.

The seriousness of marijuana use is often undermined by "more dangerous" drugs because it isn't associated with homelessness, overdose, or death the way that substances like heroin or methamphetamine are. However, marijuana can destroy lives. It happens gradually. Also, you can bet that any hard-core drug users started smoking marijuana first. Marijuana is dangerous, especially for developing brains, and is certainly a gateway to other, more lethal drugs.

Opioids

In 2015, my family and I visited Washington, DC, for the first time. My kids were ages twelve and nine, and it was a great opportunity for our family to see all of the fundamental institutions and landmarks that built America. Our first stop was Arlington National Cemetery, the final resting place of many soldiers who lost their lives fighting for our country, dating back to the Civil War. One of the most famous tombs at Arlington is the Tomb of the Unknown Soldier, which is dedicated to those who died in war and could not be identified.

Our next stop was the Lincoln Memorial, which is dedicated to one of the most beloved presidents in American history and is the place where Martin Luther King Jr. gave his famous "I Have a Dream" speech.

Next we visited the Washington Monument, followed by the Capitol building, which houses the Senate and House of Representatives. We visited many other important sites, but the one that impacted me most was the Vietnam Veterans

Memorial, because my father served in Vietnam and lost many friends in battle. The granite wall is 493.5 feet long and 10 feet high and includes the names of over 58,000 men and women killed in action. The names on the wall seemed infinite in number.

When I returned home from our trip to DC, I couldn't stop thinking about the Vietnam Veterans Memorial and how sad it was that so many young soldiers lost their lives. Then something else hit me. That same year, 2015, over 52,000 Americans lost their lives to drug overdoses, nearly the same amount of soldiers that lost their lives during the entire Vietnam War.[4]

How could this be? I wondered. Fast-forward to 2020, and the total deaths from drug overdoses eclipsed 100,000 in a one-year period, nearly double the amount from five years earlier and nearly double the amount of soldiers who died in Vietnam.[5] Drug addiction has become a national epidemic, fueled by corporate greed, economic recession, and politics.

According to an editorial in *The Lancet*, "Years of aggressive and misleading promotion by Purdue Pharma entrenched misinformation that opioids were without risk, influencing medical education and ensuring less restrictive legislation through lobbying and campaign contributions."[6] Ultimately, people were told that prescription opioids were harmless and not addictive, and as a result they didn't think twice about taking them to alleviate pain.

One of the main reasons drug overdoses have skyrocketed so fast is because of a drug known as fentanyl, a powerful synthetic opioid that is one hundred times more potent than morphine. It's a prescription medicine used to treat severe pain, but it's also made and used illegally. Drug dealers often mix fentanyl with other drugs such as cocaine and heroin because it's easy to produce and is a cheaper option. This often leads to overdose and death, as drug users aren't aware that what they are taking is so strong.

The U.S. Customs and Border Protection (CBP) recently reported that CBP officers at South Texas ports of entry have seen a significant increase in fentanyl and cocaine seizures. For fiscal year 2021, the CBP reported a 1,066 percent increase in fentanyl and a 98 percent increase in cocaine seized. By weight, 87,652 pounds of narcotics, 588 pounds of which were fentanyl, were seized, a street value close to $800 million.[7] CBP agents also reported a spike in drug trafficking offenders who have been arrested in the States, deported, and then come back without consequence.[8] Local officials are asking for more resources and stiffer penalties from the federal government.

Indeed, bad policy, corporate greed, and special interests are largely responsible for the amount of drugs entering our country and the amount of drug overdoses that ensue.

I believe marijuana is so widely used because of the same misleading policies, which are based on corporate and political greed and have subsequently desensitized our nation's youth to its dangers. Yes, I can go ask a bunch of teenagers what their thoughts are about marijuana and the majority will say it's completely harmless, but at the end of the day the influence that parents have over our children's beliefs and values cannot be matched.

We must adopt zero tolerance for all drugs, including marijuana, and we must do our best to tattoo this message on our children's brains. Will this always work? No. Many kids will still experiment with drugs they consider to be harmless, like marijuana, and if one of them is your child, you have to fight this battle. You must hold them accountable, deal with their opposition, and not give an inch.

Parent Peer Pressure

Several years ago an eighteen-year-old patient of mine developed a serious alcohol problem. His mom called me, very concerned. Her son had just started his first semester in college when he was arrested by the campus police for vandalizing parked cars while intoxicated. During our conversation, she told me that her biggest regret was allowing him to drink alcohol when he was in high school.

She told me how it started. She and her husband were very social with many parents in town. They'd met when their children were younger, through youth sports. The parents got together most weekends with their kids. At one social gathering, when the kids were sixteen, the parents who were hosting provided alcoholic beverages for the kids as well as the adults.

Quickly this became a common theme at all of the social gatherings, and although this mom was against it, she soon fell into the trap and allowed her son to also drink, since all of the other kids were allowed. She felt pressured and didn't want her son to feel left out. All of the other parents didn't think it was a big deal, since there was adult supervision. Unfortunately, her son turned out to be genetically predisposed to addiction, and eventually he had to go to rehab.

I can provide many stories like this, where parents want to be the cool parents and be friends with their kids. I saw a lot of this when my son was a senior in high school. The summer after he graduated, he attended about a dozen graduation parties. I asked him if the parents allowed the kids to drink at the parties, and he said, "Dad, are you kidding me? Not only is it allowed but the parents supply it for everyone."

I get it; the kids were all eighteen years old and were going off to college in a couple of months anyway, so what's the big deal, right? That may be the opinion many parents have, but I am not one of them. Sometimes I wonder if there's something wrong with me because I play by the rules, but I don't think so. The reason I won't supply alcohol to underage kids probably has to do with the profession I'm in—and all of the lives I've seen destroyed because of drugs and alcohol.

Remember, the younger someone starts, the more likely they are to develop an addiction. Furthermore, what if one of those underage kids were to stumble home intoxicated from a parent-run party and be killed in a car accident? Who's going to be guilty? You guessed it: the parent who hosted.

My son doesn't drink alcohol, and I'm proud of him for that. In fact, his friends, whom I've known since they were all in kindergarten, tell me that they look up to him for not drinking.

Drug and alcohol use among teenagers and adults is a serious public health issue. You can help prevent your children from falling into the hell that is addiction.

CHAPTER TIPS

- Start the conversation when your children are young. Talk to your children about the dangers and consequences of substance abuse.

- Make it clear to your children that you have zero tolerance for any form of drug use.
- Search your teen's drawers, backpacks, and phone interactions. You need to know what is going on in their lives.
- Keep an eye out for any changes you may see in your teen. If they suddenly lose interest in things or their grades drop, there's a good chance they're using marijuana.
- Don't be naïve. If you catch your teenager with a vape pen or marijuana, they'll try to minimize it and tell you that it belongs to their friend, or that they only tried it once. It's similar to the person who gets pulled over by the police and claims they only had one drink when they really had ten.
- Spend as much time as you can with your teenager. Obviously they prefer to be with friends, but make sure to have regular family dinners and other activities together. The quality time they have with you is perhaps the most important drug prevention tool there is.

Obesity and Body Image

The first book I wrote, published in 2008, was a weight-loss book entitled *Losing Weight When Diets Fail.* At the time I was using a lot of hypnotherapy with patients at my private practice as a therapeutic method to help them lose weight, which prompted me to write the book.

The book focused on applying subconscious strategies like visualization and suggestion as a tool for weight loss, which makes sense. After all, anyone who is overweight consciously knows exactly what they need to do in order to drop the pounds. They need to eat less and exercise more, but they can't do it. That's because the habits associated with weight gain are all ingrained deep inside the subconscious mind, not things that can be undone with the conscious mind. The subconscious mind is a lot more powerful than the conscious mind, and it's where all of our cravings and bad habits come from—overshadowing conscious common sense.

The subconscious mind is a supercomputer where everything is stored, including habits and cravings. You can consciously tell yourself all you want on Sunday that you are going to wake up Monday morning and go to the gym, but then you don't. That's because your subconscious mind isn't programmed to want to do that.

You may tell yourself that you're going to avoid the chocolate chip ice cream in the freezer, but then you sit down to watch television that night and it's as if there's a magnetic force coming from that freezer. It's not the ice cream in the freezer that's the magnet; it's your subconscious mental programming.

When my weight-loss book came out, I was very much involved in health and fitness both personally and professionally, and still am. I was also providing lectures to parent groups and schools to address the childhood obesity problem. One demonstration I'd give during my lectures involved the empty calories that come from sugar in sweetened soft drinks. I would explain to the audience that many kids drink as many as five servings of sweetened soft drinks on a daily basis.[1]

Then I would take out a bag of sugar and scoop forty teaspoons of sugar onto a black plastic plate to provide a visual representation of how much sugar is in five cans of soda. The forty teaspoons of sugar looked like a small mountain on that plate, and those in attendance always stared at it in disbelief.

That was fifteen years ago, and although childhood obesity was a major problem back then, it's now an epidemic. In fact, it's the number one health threat our children face. The causes of childhood obesity come down to several things: the wide variety and accessibility of packaged foods, advertising and marketing, and the sedentary lifestyle children live.

From what you've read in this book so far, I'm sure you can tell I'm not an advocate of children being indoors and not moving, staring at screens. This behavior leads to a host of mental and emotional health issues and, unfortunately, physical issues too. It's the root cause of the childhood obesity epidemic.

When a human being doesn't do all that much moving, the body doesn't do much calorie burning, and the metabolism slows down. And when children become overweight, they also become insecure, which can perpetuate anxiety, depression, and low self-esteem. Additionally, children who are obese are more likely to become adults who are obese. Adult obesity is associated with a plethora of health problems, including heart disease, type 2 diabetes, stroke, and more.

How bad is the childhood obesity epidemic? According to the Centers for Disease Control and Prevention (CDC), 33 percent of children and adolescents are overweight, and 22 percent of these overweight kids fall under the category of obese, meaning they have a body mass index (BMI) over thirty.[2] Childhood obesity alone is estimated to cost $14 billion per year in direct health expenses.

Yes, sedentary activities like watching television or using other screen devices can lead to weight gain, but children today are also getting less sleep than previous generations. This causes the gut hormone ghrelin to rise, which causes hunger and leads to cravings for junk food.

In contrast, children who eat healthy foods, are physically active, and get adequate sleep prevent the onset of chronic diseases like cancer, heart disease, and type 2 diabetes.

Fast-Food Nation

The fast-food industry is a huge factor in this burgeoning epidemic, and in recent years it has exploded. When I was a kid, there was only one fast-food joint in town. Now we see fast-food restaurants on every corner. Have you taken a long drive on a highway recently? I have. I've taken many twelve-hour drives to visit relatives and my son at college, and along the route are signs at every exit for restaurants like McDonald's, Burger King, Chipotle, Chick-fil-A, and many more. It's unbelievable how many of these places there are.

The growth of the fast-food industry has made high-fat, inexpensive meals available throughout the world, and quantity has become a major selling point. Just look at the names the fast-food chains give to their burgers. McDonald's sells the Big Mac, Wendy's offers the Big Classic, and Burger King lures you in with the Whopper. What do all of these names make you think of? Size, of course.

According to Eric Schlosser, author of *Fast Food Nation: The Dark Side of the All-American Meal*, a large soda at most fast-food restaurants is as large as 32 ounces and has 310 calories![3] When I was a kid, a large soda at McDonald's was 16 ounces. Back then, kids drank an average of about 8 ounces of soda a day. Today they drink an average of 24 ounces—three times as much! In fact, kids today drink twice as much soda as they do milk.[4]

In *Fast Food Nation*, Schlosser also talks about how the fast-food industry makes promotional deals with leading toy makers, giving away simple toys with their kids' meals and selling higher profile toys at a discount. It's a clever way to target kids. A successful toy promotion can double or triple the weekly sales volume of children's meals.

The fast-food industry spends five billion dollars a year on advertising, and most of it is done subliminally, meaning that the commercials and ads affect you without your conscious recognition. You may notice the contents of a commercial, but you probably don't realize it's directed toward that uncritical subconscious mind I mentioned. The purpose of advertising is to hit you where it hurts: emotionally.

Recently, I watched a particular fast-food commercial that showed a mom and young daughter eating burgers and fries together during the mother's lunch break from work. It seemed innocent enough, but here's what the real message was: the mother was dressed in a business suit and had a briefcase, and the young girl told her mom she appreciated spending quality time with her. The mom guiltily looked at her daughter while they both smiled and ate their French fries.

A working mother watching this commercial would subconsciously absorb the message and feel guilty without even realizing it. She would feel compelled to take her child to a fast-food restaurant without consciously knowing why. Most people would agree that this kind of brainwashing exists, but in the entire history of humankind, no one who has ever been brainwashed has realized it at the time.

Because eating makes you feel good, over time you learn to associate happiness and feeling good with food. This is one of the main reasons people overeat, including kids. When you're stressed or unhappy, your mind produces hunger signals because it wants to replace stressful feelings with feelings of pleasure. In your mind, food is equated with pleasure.

It acts like a painkiller. When the painkiller wears off, the unpleasant feelings return, and you need to take another one.

For most people, food has become a powerful remedy for emotional discomfort. When we feel stressed or unhappy, we turn to food to fill the void. If we're lonely, a bag of chips can be our best friend. If we're unhappy, chocolate can heal the pain. It's become second nature for most people to pair food with feelings in this way and not even realize it. It isn't healthy or natural. *It's natural to eat when you feel hungry, to eat slowly, and to enjoy your food in moderation.* It's not natural to eat if you're not hungry, and it's not natural to quickly stuff your mouth with everything in sight.

When you experience emotional pain, there's always an empty feeling inside; something is missing. Food can become the substance that numbs the pain and fills the emptiness. It temporarily relieves the uncomfortable feelings or circumstances. But the relief is only temporary. It doesn't solve emotional problems. It makes them worse.

As we struggle to balance the responsibilities of life and find ourselves coping with nonstop stress, fatigue, and worry, we may automatically reach for food to blunt the pain without even realizing it.

As the mental health epidemic continues to swirl out of control for our kids, food can become the ultimate painkiller. Like the tech industry, the food industry couldn't give a hoot about children's well-being. They care about one thing: the almighty dollar.

I highly recommend that you read the Rudd Center report about fast-food advertising to children and teens. You can find it in the notes in the back of the book.[5]

According to the report, one-third of children and teens eat fast food on any given day, and consume up to 310 additional calories on the days they do. Fast-food consumption is higher for Hispanic and Black teens, who already face a greater risk for obesity compared to White teens. Consumption of fast food has increased over the last ten years among children and teens, and one of the main reasons is extensive advertising. In fact, fast food is the most frequently advertised food and beverage category directed toward children and teens, making up 40 percent of all youth-directed food marketing expenditures. Widespread exposure to all of this advertising influences preferences, consumption, and attitudes about unhealthy fast food.

The writers of the report believe that limiting fast-food marketing to youth is a key public health strategy to address the poor diet among kids. The good news is that some fast-food restaurants have responded to public health concerns by adding healthier menu items. Others have pledged to advertise only healthier items to children, but it's still unknown if they have done so. Some of the key items uncovered in the report are as follows:

- In 2019, children and teens viewed on average 2.1 to 2.3 fast-food TV ads per day promoting regular menu items and also promoting the restaurant itself.
- In 2019, fast-food restaurants spent $318 million to advertise on Spanish-language TV, a 33 percent increase from 2012.
- In 2019, Black preschoolers, children, and teens viewed 75 percent more fast-food related ads than their White peers.

127

- A total of 274 fast-food restaurants advertised in 2019, and six of them (McDonald's, Domino's, Burger King, Taco Bell, Sonic, and Little Caesars) were responsible for 46 percent of all fast-food ad spending.

Here's another interesting fact from the report: the amount of time that teenagers spent watching television *decreased* between 2012 and 2019. Remember, 2012 is when the smartphone became mainstream, which led to a decline in TV ads viewed. As a result, extensive fast-food marketing on social media, influencer marketing, product placements, sponsorships, and other newer forms of marketing have ensued. All of this new marketing is designed to disproportionally reach and appeal to children and teens. Great—more bad things we can add to the list of stuff polluting our children's brains.

Although restaurant corporate offices have promised to create initiatives to offer more nutritious options and provide support for racial justice, their promises haven't included improving their unhealthy marketing practices that are aimed at communities of color. Thankfully, there's much effort among municipalities and states to enact legislation that will help improve kids' meal nutrition.

It seems that just about everything regarding our children's health, whether physical or mental, is associated with screen time. The more time our children spend online and on social media, the more exposure they have to ads from fast-food makers, and the more likely they are to become obese. And it's not just because of the repetitive messages of juicy, flame-broiled burgers penetrating their subconscious minds and causing cravings. When they're on their screens they're sedentary; there's no physical movement. It is a double whammy.

A married couple I was working with at my private practice had a twelve-year-old daughter who was causing a lot of issues in the family. She was explosive and disrespectful, and the parents had reached their wits' end. I worked with the girl both individually and together with her parents. Each week she would come to my office right after school and would always have two bags of barbecue potato chips and a 20-ounce bottle of soda. The chips weren't the single-serving bags that you buy in bulk, either, but rather the bigger 2½-ounce bags. She would scarf down both bags and the soda.

I remember wondering how the girl could possibly eat dinner when she got home. Well, she didn't. She'd often refuse to eat the dinners her mom prepared, which was causing even more conflict in the family. After working with the family for a time, I learned that the mom was too nice. She loved her daughter very much but also enabled her and pretty much gave her whatever she wanted because she always wanted to please her.

It's understandable. We all love our kids and want them to be happy, but this mom went a bit over the top. I told her she needed to stop pleasing her daughter all the time because she was becoming an entitled little brat, which was part of the reason for her disrespectful behavior. I had to help the mom step out of her comfort zone and start putting her foot down, because her daughter was walking all over her.

Thankfully, she did. She stopped giving her daughter money to buy junk food and stopped filling the cabinets with whatever her daughter wanted. She stopped constantly pleasing her and started parenting her. And the daughter's behavior gradually improved. Furthermore, the mom was able to curb her daughter's poor eating habits and reduce her risk of becoming unhealthy and overweight.

Physical Activity

Earlier I talked about green time—being outdoors—and how important it is for children's mental well-being. It's also important for children's physical well-being.

In 1984, when I was twelve years old, the percentage of obese kids in America was only 1.5 percent, compared to 22 percent today. It's not like we were starved. I ate plenty of McDonald's (albeit in smaller portions). Kids were slimmer because we were much more active. Certainly there's a larger selection of processed foods and fast food today, and that doesn't help, but there's a lot to be said about kids riding bikes and playing outside, something we don't see as much of today.

Hopefully, we can bring biking back. One organization is trying. All Kids Bike is a national movement to place learn-to-ride programs in public schools through donations from individuals, businesses, and organizations. They ship free bikes and equipment to schools, and kindergarten students learn how to ride. PE teachers access simple training and then receive a program certification. It's that simple. Their goal is to reduce childhood obesity, screen time, and inactivity as well as increase play, socialization, and academic performance. They also provide some fantastic statistics about the benefits of riding bikes.[6]

- The more children play outdoors, the less likely they are to be obese. Higher levels of outdoor play, like biking, lead to a 42 percent reduction in a child's risk of obesity.

- Overweight adolescents who participate in bicycling three to four times per week are 85 percent more likely to become normal-weight adults.

- Children who walk or bike to school starting at an early age are more likely to stay at a healthy weight during their school years.

- Regular exercise, including biking, reduces depression and improves self-esteem in overweight children.

- Kids who exercise, biking included, have a higher level of self-confidence and self-esteem. Exercise also improves academic performance and socialization skills.

- Play enhances brain structure and promotes executive functions.

- Kids who are active are more physically confident and therefore more likely to be active and healthy adults.

- Evidence shows that physical activity not only improves grades but also improves standardized test scores.

Another initiative to help tackle childhood obesity and improve the overall well-being of children is BOKS (Build Our Kids' Success).

In today's screen obsessed culture, kids are the least active generation in history. The sedentary lifestyle is negatively impacting both their physical, mental and social health. BOKS is a physical activity program designed to reverse this public health crisis by getting kids active and establishing a lifelong commitment to health and fitness.[7]

Created by the Reebok Canada Fitness Foundation and the Public Health Agency of Canada, BOKS incorporates physical activity and play as a tool to keep kids happy and healthy, especially during times of adversity. The program started with a single elementary school and has grown into a global initiative that "envisions a world in which movement is a foundational part of every child's day." The program is typically delivered in-person, at schools and youth organizations, and offers physical activity plans for teachers and volunteers to help kids stay active while they are at home and combat the isolated, sedentary nature of screen time.

Dalhousie University conducted research about the effectiveness of the program by interviewing BOKS students, parents, and program leaders. They found that after two months of BOKS participation, children experienced

- a significant decrease in psychological distress and sleep disturbance;
- improvements in peer relationships, cognitive function, and life satisfaction; and
- noticeable changes in mood, behavior, and ability to resolve conflict.[8]

Body Image

Although childhood obesity is a serious problem, there's another physical issue affecting our children's health. It's called body image. Body image is how you see yourself when you look in the mirror and also how you see yourself in your mind. Remember, your mind is very powerful and impressionable. The effects of social media on teenagers' body image are well documented. In September 2021, a *Wall Street Journal* article revealed that Facebook, owner of Instagram, knew their platform made teen girls feel worse about their bodies.[9] They conducted their own internal research, became aware of this problem, and buried it. A whistleblower then came forward, and the story blew up very quickly.

Consumer Reports conducted their own research on this matter and found that social media use can have negative emotional effects.[10] A nationally representative survey conducted in August 2021 found that 26 percent of people who ever had a social media account said they felt jealous or bad after looking at someone else's social media posts.

The envy we often feel about others' lives while scrolling through TikTok, Instagram, or Facebook can quickly become destructive, particularly for young people, often affecting their self-worth and warping their self-image. Celebrity images, social media influencer images, and even images of friends flaunting their abs and perfect bodies can really get to people's heads, especially young girls, and cause questions to arise in their minds. *Am I good enough? Could I ever look like that? Should I go on a diet?*

According to Dr. Arpan Parikh, a psychiatrist who was interviewed by *Consumer Reports*, "When you're obsessed with your body image or are anxiety-ridden about a specific part of your body, and then feel a compulsion to act on that obsession, that's body dysmorphia, an obsessive-compulsive disorder rooted in anxiety."[11]

133

This can happen very quickly and can lead people down a dark path. It can often result in anorexia or bulimia, which are eating disorders characterized by low body weight and a heightened fear of gaining weight. People with either of these conditions become obsessed with their shape and weight and go to extreme measures to control it, thereby causing a significant impact on their life and their health. Eating disorders tend to be associated with teenage girls, but they also affect boys.

A recent peer-reviewed study showed a 15 percent increase in eating disorder diagnoses in 2020 compared to previous years among people under age thirty.[12] While most of the research on diagnosing eating disorders focused on females, new research suggests that males may now account for half of all eating disorder cases. There is a relatively new type of eating disorder known as avoidant restrictive food intake disorder, which involves inadequate food intake but doesn't include distress about body shape or image like anorexia or bulimia. It's most common in male athletes who diet, skip meals, and are obsessed with exercising. The signs that a youth may be developing eating disorder behaviors include working out more than is advised by a coach or trainer, avoiding eating in public, being hyperfocused on "clean" eating, and using steroids, diet pills, or laxatives.

Indeed, obesity and body image are both public health crises that we can add to the ever-growing issues our children face. Fortunately, there's plenty we can do to help prevent these issues and address them, including simple strategies you can begin to implement in your own family today.

CHAPTER TIPS

- Make sure your children are active. Get them out the front door, get them a bike, do something. Physical movement is a child's birthright.
- Ensure that your children get adequate sleep. Kids are sleeping less hours per night nowadays, mainly because they have their phones in their bedrooms. Set a strict bedtime and make sure the phone is removed from their bedroom one hour before they go to bed.
- Buy healthier food. Many families I've worked with express concerns about children who are either over-weight or have poor eating habits—but they are the ones buying their children the cookies and chips. Replace junk foods with healthier options, like fruits and vegetables. Your child will complain at first but will eventually get used it.
- If you notice that your teen has become obsessed with clean eating or working out, intervene early. Have a conversation with them and explain that working out and eating healthily are both good things, but it is a problem if they become an obsession.

School and Learning

So far I've outlined many challenges our children face in the modern world and what we can do to help them navigate these obstacles. The ever-changing education system in America poses another set of challenges for our children.

First, modern technology has replaced paper and pencil learning with computers and tablets, and many of today's kids don't know how to write with a pencil because they have never needed to. Although computer-based learning provides students with tremendous access to all sorts of innovative information, it's also the biggest source of student distraction. Many children—whether sitting in the classroom or doing homework in their bedroom—cannot resist the temptation to switch from tab to tab and check their social media feeds, watch videos, or play games. This affects their ability to focus and retain important information.

Another change in education is remote learning, something that was necessary in the 2020–21 school year because of the pandemic. This is a topic that will be talked about well into the future. The learning curve that remote learning presented to both students and teachers was not a one-size-fits-all approach. Some students welcomed the change while others struggled with it. Many parents were not happy with how public schools handled education during the pandemic and opted for private school and homeschooling.

Lastly, public schools have had to focus on students' mental health more than ever before. Rates of anxiety, depression, and suicide have reached epidemic proportions. Naturally, schools should do all they can to help students with mental health issues, but there's no denying that the mental health crisis has an impact on education.

The big question is, Are these changes to the structure of America's education system helping our children and preparing them for college and the workforce?

A History of Education

In 1875, Congress passed an amendment that mandated free public education for all. This was an important step for equality in education for all people, regardless of socioeconomic background. In the early part of the twentieth century, poorer children were forced to work, which kept them out of school. The government then passed child labor laws that prohibited children from working, which enabled more children to attend school, particularly poorer children.

By 1917, every state in the union had passed mandatory educational laws, meaning that every child in America was required to attend school. Every town and city was required to provide free schooling for all. During the Great Depression of the 1930s, as public bus lines closed, poorer students who didn't have access to private transportation struggled to get to school. School bus transportation was then created, making it easier for children to get to school.

Then, in the 1950s, school segregation was abolished and it became unconstitutional to segregate students based on race. It might be hard to believe that segregation was legal not so long ago, but it was.

As times progressed, things like the School Breakfast Program, Title IX, the Americans with Disabilities Act, No Child Left Behind, and Common Core were all enacted. Then came the STEM movement in 2013, followed by the Race to the Top initiative and then remote learning. Presently, computer-based learning is at the forefront of education.

Computer Learning and Virtual Learning

The pros and cons of technology in the classroom are debated every time new technology enters the classroom. Computer technology—in and out of the classroom—is here to stay and will only continue to advance in coming years. When I think back to my own schooling, I remember the green chalkboards and the irritating sound the chalk made as my teachers wrote on that board. I have memories of lugging home large textbooks, along with the dent in my finger from being forced to write in cursive, with a pencil, for what felt like hours at a time. My own kids didn't have any of these experiences. What they will remember are smartboards, projectors, laptops, and iPads.

One of the advantages of using computer technology in the classroom is that teachers can identify each student's style of learning and adjust their teaching accordingly. Because technology is a part of just about every aspect of our children's lives, teachers can utilize various apps and websites for educational purposes.

There are also countless online education platforms available to teachers that provide immediate feedback about how each student is performing, allowing teachers to quickly see the performance level of each student and identify any problem areas they may encounter. Classroom technology is an excellent feedback mechanism.

Another advantage of modern technology in learning is that it can be used for group collaboration. Students can work together through their devices, which often improves group problem-solving and participation.

However, there are downsides. Computer-based learning often leads to distractibility, because kids are always looking to entertain themselves with their devices, especially when they're at home working on group projects. Because kids interact with their peers more often through their devices than they do face-to-face, it can also negatively affect social skills. There has to be a balance between face-to-face interaction and device-to-device interaction, both in and out of the classroom.

When the pandemic hit in March 2020, school districts across the country had to scramble to purchase netbooks and other devices for kids to use at home because schools were shut down. When schools reopened, many still relied heavily on technology, which isn't good news for younger students. Many elementary-age students have become accustomed to learning through their devices, which concerns many experts because it's imperative that children learn to read and write first and use computers later.

Preadolescents tend to be easily distracted by computers and other screen devices and struggle to attend to their teacher. Younger children are also easily stimulated by computers and devices, which can have a negative impact on their reading skills and decrease their working memory.

Another basic skill that's essential for younger children to develop is delayed gratification, as I talked about earlier. When children can quickly google an answer to something rather than reading a book to find the answer, they get accustomed to the instant feedback, which can lead to struggling with activities that require effort and time.

Distractibility is another commonality among teens. Not only do they rely heavily on computers for school, but many are addicted to social media and other forms of technology, which distracts them as they study and do homework, thereby interrupting learning. A former patient of mine named Lenny is an example.

Lenny was a sixteen-year-old boy who was having issues with his father. His parents were divorced, and he didn't see his father often. When he did see him, his father would often lose his temper. Lenny longed to have a strong father/ son relationship with his dad, but didn't. This bothered him a lot, and he often thought about what he missed growing up without his father there.

During one of our sessions, Lenny told me that he was having difficulty focusing and concentrating at school and while doing his homework. He couldn't figure out why. We explored what was going on. Were the issues with his father weighing on his mind and causing him to be distracted? Or was it something else?

I asked Lenny if he spent a lot of time on his phone, and he told me that he didn't. I then asked if I could see his phone. I discovered that Lenny was spending eight hours per day, on average, on his phone. Most of these hours were spent scrolling through TikTok videos. Lenny was absolutely shocked. He had no idea he was spending that much time on his phone. This was what was causing his distractibility, and I challenged him to delete TikTok from his phone, which he did. His grades quickly improved.

The biggest computer-based learning setback I witnessed happened during the pandemic when schools were required to close their doors, and bedrooms and kitchens became the new classrooms for millions of kids. Kids were required to log on to their computers in the morning, and their teachers taught them through their computer screens. This caused lots of issues, because many kids weren't able to concentrate and stay on task for that many consecutive hours on a computer.

Although some of the kids I counseled during the pandemic preferred remote learning and did well with it, most did not. In fact, the majority of kids I spoke with during the pandemic wanted to go back to school in person again. In the beginning of the pandemic, remote learning sounded great to kids. It was like an extended snow day. It meant they could stay up later and sleep in later. They also wouldn't have to commute to school. But the excitement didn't last long.

A lot of working parents during the pandemic had no choice but to leave their high schoolers on their own, cross their fingers, and hope that their teenage sons and daughters would be responsible. They were expected to get up, log on to their computers, and do school—but like I mentioned earlier, kids, especially teenagers, aren't always responsible by nature.

Several teenagers I counseled at the time told me they would set their alarms to wake them up literally a minute or two before virtual school started. Groggily, they would log on while still in their beds, where they would remain for the entire virtual school day, in their pajamas. Others told me they weren't required to have their computer cameras turned on during virtual school, so they would quickly log on, turn off the camera, and go back to sleep. There was no way for their teachers to know.

Still others told me that it didn't matter if they slept through their virtual classes because it was easy to cheat and get decent grades. The problem was they didn't learn anything. Those students who were required to have their camera turned on and took school seriously told me they didn't learn very much either, because the teachers made it too easy. Lastly, other kids I counseled, though also required to have their cameras turned on, would often open their You-Tube or Netflix tabs and watch videos and movies instead of listening to their teachers' lectures. There was no way the teachers could tell.

Perhaps the most severe case of computer/remote learning gone bad that I witnessed was with a teenage patient I was counseling who suffered from school phobia. When it was announced that his school had shut down and would be all virtual, it sounded like the greatest thing that could ever happen to him, because it meant he no longer had to

143

worry about his attendance. His mother was also relieved, because her son's school avoidance weighed heavily on her.

Unfortunately, it didn't go well. He and a group of his friends decided to take advantage of the remote-learning arrangements. They played video games straight through the night and into the morning. At 8:00 a.m. they would log on to virtual school without having slept the night before. When the virtual school day ended at 2:00 p.m., they all went to bed. This became their new academic routine, which completely threw off their sleep schedules and affected them in other ways. It's hard to believe that the parents of these kids allowed this. I think it was because they felt bad because kids at that time weren't allowed to see each other in person, and this was the only way they could socialize.

Technology and remote learning certainly have their place in education, but as you can see it isn't perfect. It's up to us to closely monitor what our children are doing when they have a screen in front of them that they're supposed to be using exclusively for school. Too many kids can't resist the temptation of wandering off to social media or gaming sites.

School closure mandates that led to at-home virtual learning alternatives, although useful for some, weren't useful for the majority. And because private schools were not required to resort to virtual schooling, a new shift in education began: an increase in private school attendance as well as homeschooling.

The Shift from Public Education

When the majority of public schools in America went virtual in 2020, public school enrollment dropped precipitously. According to Kerry McDonald, author of *Unschooled: Raising Curious, Well-Educated Children Outside the Conventional Classroom*, in 2020 private school enrollment increased, and homeschooling education tripled from its pre-pandemic levels.[1]

Major cities like Los Angeles, Chicago, and Seattle saw some of the largest public school enrollment drops. Los Angeles public school enrollment, for example, dropped 4.76 percent in the 2020–21 school year. One might assume that in 2021, when public schools began providing in-person learning again, parents would've been eager to reenroll their children in their local school districts. That wasn't the case.

According to McDonald, data showed that the enrollment in Los Angeles public schools was down 27,000 students in the fall of 2021, an additional 6 percent drop from the previous school year. Furthermore, Seattle saw 1,300 students exit the public school system and opt for either private school or homeschool. The Seattle public school system lost approximately $28 million in state funding as a result. McDonald believes that the shift away from public schooling is likely to be long lasting and will have substantial effects on funding.[2]

So, what happened? Parents became frustrated by the back and forth school closure mandates and saw firsthand the lack of effectiveness that virtual schooling provided. Even after public schools appeared to reopen for good, parents could never be sure if leaders would shut them down again.

McDonald also believes that funding bureaucratic school systems rather than allowing government education dollars to flow toward school choice, vouchers, and scholarship programs is also part of the reason for the exodus, considering that nearly three-quarters of US taxpayers support school choice policies. McDonald is a strong supporter of private education and homeschooling and believes we need to weaken the government's monopoly position on education because doing so will encourage a flourishing free market of learning opportunities for our children. The theory is this would allow for greater creativity, possibility, and efficiency. It's starting to happen already, as entrepreneurs have stepped in to create new schooling alternatives and learning models that offer variety, personalization, and flexibility.

Private School Surge

Beginning in March 2020, just about every school in the country, public and private, closed their doors to in-person learning for the remainder of the school year because of the pandemic. At the start of the following school year, when many private schools went back to in-person learning and most public schools continued with remote learning, remote schooling was not an option for many parents who would have to juggle work and childcare. So they began enrolling their children in private school.

According to Dr. Karen Aronian, a parenting and education expert, "parents opted for and enrolled their children in private schools for 'in-person school certainty.'"[3] Although parents had to pay for their kids to attend private schools, many of them thought it was worth it. Private schools recognized the necessity of keeping their paying clientele happy and "worked from a place of yes" to make school happen, said Aronian. Ultimately, parents recognized that when you are a paying school customer, your opinion (and money) matters.

Additionally, many families who chose private school recognized added benefits such as access to more robust learning, smaller class sizes, and a more customized, personalized curriculum.[4]

Although private school comes with a huge price tag, and paying for it has affected many parents' college funding plans and retirement plans, it was a trade-off they were willing to make because their children were able to continue to learn seamlessly in person while avoiding the pitfalls and stresses of virtual learning.

Catholic schools also benefited immensely from the pandemic, with enrollment jumping 3.8 percent, the first enrollment increase after decades of declining enrollment. Catholic schools enrolled an additional 62,000 students in 2021, with more than half of the enrollment increase, 66 percent, attributed to pre-kindergarten enrollment, which saw a 34 percent increase. States that were less likely to have in-person learning saw the highest increases in Catholic school enrollment, with California showing a 134 percent increase and Utah 137 percent.[5]

Homeschooling

Homeschooling has also surged in the United States. In the 2020–21 school year, homeschooling increased to 11.1 percent of total US students, up from 5.4 percent the previous school year.[6] According to Dr. Stephen Duvall, Director of Research for the Home School Legal Defense Association, a nonprofit organization, the public school population may not return to its former levels for years to come.[7]

Duvall believes one reason for the surge in homeschooling

stems from parental dissatisfaction with the quality of ac-ademic instruction that occurs in schools. One report re-vealed that students lost five months in academic gain in mathematics and four months in reading during the 2020–21 pandemic-affected school year. When coupled with recent reports concerning parental dissatisfaction with some con-troversial subjects inserted into school curriculum, it seemed reasonable that more parents were opting for homeschool-ing, says Duvall.[8]

One of the benefits of homeschooling is that parents get to choose the curriculum that best suits their children's needs, and there is an abundance of curricula in the marketplace. Additionally, in many states homeschoolers are no longer required to submit testing for the public schools, which is something many parents opposed when Common Core came into effect.

Although some parents are concerned that homeschooling can lead to a lack of social interaction, many homeschool par-ents would disagree with this notion. Because homeschooled children don't have to switch classes for seven or eight hours a day, they often have more social interaction than public school kids because there's more time available to do so.

Additionally, many homeschooling parents connect with other homeschoolers in their community and arrange ac-tivities and social events for their children. Others arrange physical education classes and field trips together.

Homeschooling isn't for everyone, but it's certainly some-thing to consider. It's a big decision and responsibility, but the good news is that if you try homeschooling your children and it doesn't go as planned, you can always transfer them back to their public school at any time.

Mental Health in Schools

In addition to these educational changes and debatable topics, there's another school issue affecting our children that I believe is the biggest one of all: mental health. During my final year as a public high school counselor in 2020, a friend of mine asked me what it was like working at a school then compared to earlier in my career. I told him that schools had become part academic and part mental health institutes. In my first years as a counselor, we didn't have a lot of mental health crises occurring in the school compared to today. In a short period of time, I went from having a handful of mental health crises per year to a handful per day.

The mental health epidemic seemed to come out of nowhere, and schools now are required to deal with it on a daily basis. It all started in 2012, when smartphones became mainstream. I explain all of this in *Disconnected*, so you should read that book. But for now, I want to talk about some of the necessary changes that have taken place in school counseling departments to help address the mental health crisis.

The Early Days in School Counseling

When I graduated college with a psychology degree in 1994, we were in the middle of a recession and the job market wasn't great, so I wasn't sure what I was going to do. My father was a police officer and highly revered for the work he was doing in a local school district at the time. It was a vocational high school district with three campuses that served the entire county.

He started a program for the school district called the "police liaison program," which connected at-risk students with police officers who acted as mentors. He became close with all of the administrators and counselors in the school district and became especially close with the schools' substance awareness coordinator (SAC). At the time, I had heard of guidance counselors and school psychologists but had never heard of SACs.

I began doing some research into the SAC certification, and it turned out to be a relatively new position that the New Jersey Department of Education had certificated in the early '90s to help combat youth addiction, which had become a real problem. It turned out that the school district my dad worked closely with was looking to hire two more SACs so that they had one at each campus.

After I completed the necessary requirements for certification, I was hired by the school district and started working for them two months later. My job dealt specifically with substance abuse prevention, intervention, and referral services. Among other things, I ran groups, hired speakers, and connected students with rehabilitation facilities.

After six years with that school district, I accepted a job at another high school, where I worked for nineteen more years until I retired in 2020. About halfway through my career, the New Jersey Department of Education changed the name of the position to student assistance counselor, and the requirements for the SAC certification also changed to include a forty-eight-credit master's degree.

The reason for the changes to the title and scope of the position was because SACs were doing a lot more than just handling substance abuse issues. We had become quasi school therapists because of the increasing mental health issues that were occurring. During my twenty-five years as a SAC, the majority of public high schools and middle schools in New Jersey employed SACs. Those that didn't were encouraged to hire them, because the mental health crisis was progressively getting worse.

In November 2021 I was speaking to a former colleague of mine, the director of guidance at a nearby high school. I was very familiar with her school's counseling department, which included her, six guidance counselors, and a SAC. The school served approximately one thousand students. She told me that the school had recently revamped its entire counseling department because they simply couldn't handle the number of students in need of mental health services. They now had two departments under the counseling department umbrella, a guidance department and a wellness department. The new wellness department was staffed with five people: the director, two SACs, and two nurses. It was created to bridge the physical and mental health needs of students.

If you think back to your own experience as a student, you likely remember having a guidance counselor who was available to help you with scheduling, college searches, and sometimes just a shoulder to lean on. Clearly that has changed, as schools need to be more equipped to handle not only students' academic needs but also the burden of mental health needs.

All in all, the landscape of education has changed dramatically in America. Students must deal with the endless distractions from their handheld devices, laptops, and tablets. Politics has become a focal point of our society and has made its way into the educational system, often causing confusion and conflict for many students and parents. Parents have had to adjust to the back-and-forth of school closures and virtual learning, along with handling controversial issues like possible vaccine mandates. Many are opting for privatized schooling and homeschooling.

Parents and schools alike must endure the unprecedented mental health issues that children today face, and many like myself just wish we could rewind the clock and go back to the way things were in the past, but that isn't possible. Instead, we need to continue to love and support our children. We must guide them with our own morals and values, and we must be there for them at every turn. Doing so will move the clock forward to a place of progress and mental wellness rather than mental decline. We have options, folks. If your children are struggling with all that modern education has become, there's a lot that you can do.

—————— CHAPTER TIPS ——————

- If your children are flourishing in school and are happy, don't change a thing. Instead continue to encourage your children and be grateful.
- Know what is being taught in your children's school. Attend school board meetings and respectfully ask questions.
- If you're unhappy with the education your children are receiving, research private schools in your area and homeschooling alternatives. If you don't have the financial means to pursue these options, reach out to

these schools anyway. You'd be surprised how many offer scholarships based on financial need.

- Talk to your children about anything and everything, and know what your children are learning. Remember, their values and morals must come from you and not anyone else.
- If a child is struggling mentally, reach out to your school's counseling department. Many of these departments are now equipped with highly trained counselors who are prepared to help you and your children.

College Admissions Pressure and Debt

In May of my senior year in high school, I had no idea if
or where I was going to college. I was a decent student,
but since neither of my parents had the opportunity to
attend college, I didn't have much direction about the application process, cost, and so on. I also never met my guidance
counselor in high school.

My older brother was the first in our family to attend
college. He attended Manhattan College in New York City,
so I decided to apply there as well. I was also recruited to
play baseball at St. Thomas Aquinas College, a small, local
college I had no interest in attending.

After I was accepted to Manhattan College, my dad sat me
down and told me he couldn't afford to send me there because

the tuition was nearly twice that of St. Thomas Aquinas. Although I was disappointed that I would have to attend St. Thomas Aquinas College as a commuter student, I understood my father's predicament. I had tremendous respect for how hard he worked and everything he did for my siblings and me.

When I had completed my first two years at St. Thomas Aquinas, I had no interest in transferring. I'd made a lot of friends and was doing well on the baseball team. When I look back, attending St. Thomas Aquinas was the right decision. I suppose I could've taken out loans and attended a fancier, name-brand college, but I didn't know anything about that process back then. My naïveté worked to my advantage. Today, I love my career and wouldn't change a thing. I'd be in the same place I am now regardless of where I attended college.

After I graduated St. Thomas Aquinas and got my first full-time job working at the vocational school, I continued attending graduate school in the evenings, part-time. I selected a local state university because it was much more affordable, and I was able to pay the tuition in full each semester, leaving myself with zero debt.

College Savings Done Right

When my wife and I were married in 1997, we rented an apartment in Palisades Park. During our time there, I learned some impressive things about her, including that she was an under-spender and an over-saver.

After six years in Palisades Park, we'd saved a nice chunk of change and were able to make a sizable down payment on a house that I hadn't thought we'd be able to afford. I have no idea how, but we paid off the mortgage in five years. When we moved into the house in March 2003 my wife was seven months pregnant with our first child, Matthew, who was born two months later.

While we were having dinner one evening not long after, my wife explained the importance of saving for Matthew's college education. I remember thinking to myself, *We are going to start saving now? That seems pretty early*. But she was right, and we set up a 529 college savings account. The account included a credit card perk that would put 2 percent of all credit card purchases into the 529 account. So, for example, if our credit card bill was $3,000 that month, we would receive $60 free money that would be deposited into the 529 account. It might not sound like much, but it added up over time.

During that conversation over dinner, my wife said that our goal should be to put $1,000 a month into the 529 account and that every purchase we made, from gas to groceries to furniture, should be made with that credit card so we could benefit from the additional 2 percent. Of course, that meant being able to pay off the credit card each month in order to avoid paying interest, which we did.

Although we were earning more money after six years of marriage and were both nearing thirty years old, I still didn't see how we would be able to do this, but we did. We lived a comfortable life but were very smart about what we purchased and how we saved. We looked through the newspaper circulars on Sundays and cut out grocery store coupons. We purchased our cars and drove them until they were no longer drivable. Having no car payments freed up money for us to reach our college savings goals and other financial goals.

In 2006 our second child, Ashlyn, was born, and that meant another child to save for. It also meant that my wife quit her job to stay home with the kids. We were one salary down, so I did what I've always done—I worked my butt off. I worked at the high school, earned my professional counseling license, and had a part-time private counseling practice going as planned. I'll admit that I felt some financial pressure with my wife not working outside the home, but we continued to stretch every dollar, live below our means, and save.

In August 2021, I dropped my son off at Clemson University in South Carolina, where he is currently studying chemical engineering. Although he was accepted to some "more prestigious" private schools in the northeast, he chose Clemson because it was the perfect feel and the perfect fit.

Prestige Pressure

Kids today experience tremendous pressure when it comes to college applications and admissions. Senior year in high school is wrought with a never-ending checklist designed to showcase excellence. Letters of recommendation, essays, GPAs, standardized test scores, volunteer hours, and extracurricular activities are all tabulated to match students to the college that's the best and most prestigious fit.

It's emotionally and mentally exhausting for high school seniors, and for many of them not being accepted to their dream school would be a failure. The unhealthy message directed at students by some college admissions committees is that they must do whatever it takes, at any cost, if they want to be "accepted" to that prestigious institution, even if that means crafting an application that isn't consistent with their real passions and goals.

The truth is that what a student does while they are in college is much more important than the name of the college they attend. However, the Ivy League and other elite institutions have many of us believing that attending their school is the golden ticket to success. I don't want to downplay those colleges, as they can certainly give students a leg up when applying for their first job, but after young adults enter the workforce, experience and work ethic are more important than the college they attended when it comes to advancing in their careers.

My nephew is an example. He attended Quinnipiac University in Connecticut, where he majored in finance. Quinnipiac is a good school but not an eyebrow raiser like Harvard or Stanford. My nephew worked very hard in college, was the head of the finance club, and networked with everyone he could. He wound up with three job offers from reputable companies in New York City. After three years at his first job, he had an opportunity to apply for an opening at another financial institution. There were over one hundred other applicants, and after several interviews it came down to him and two Ivy League graduates. My nephew got the job.

Debt Crisis

According to researchers at Education Data Initiative, Americans owe a total of $1.75 trillion in federal and private student loans.[1] This student loan debt crisis affects over 43 million Americans and has prompted legislative action for the first time in the federal student loan program history.

Fully 15 percent of American adults have outstanding undergraduate student loan debt, and 12.4 percent of student loan debt in repayment is delinquent. As unpaid debts continue to accrue interest, paying back those loans becomes less likely. For example, the average 1996 college graduate owed $12,750 in student loans, and those who still had loans remaining ten years later owed an average of $16,550, which is $22,110 in 2021 dollars.

Education Data Initiative researchers explain that borrowers who fall behind on their payments suffer substantial consequences, as it impacts their credit score, thereby affecting their ability to get an automobile loan, a mortgage, or another loan to pursue a higher degree. Essentially, they fall into a debt spiral that affects all areas of their lives. Some of the other data the researchers found is equally disheartening.

- Student loan debt has outpaced rising tuition costs by 353.8 percent.
- $90.5 million of debt was delinquent in the first fiscal quarter of 2020.
- Collective student debt increased 8.28 percent in 2020.
- 15.1 percent of student borrowers under forty years old are behind on their payments.
- Twenty years after entering school, half of student borrowers still owe $20,000 on their outstanding loan balances.
- 11.8 percent of delinquent loan debt is in default.[2]

The student loan debt crisis is so bad that economists compare it to the housing bubble and subprime mortgage calamity during the 2007–09 recession. Experts point to excessive federal lending as a main contributing factor to the crisis, which started in 1978. The Middle Income Student Assistance Act (MISAA) of 1978 made federal student loans more accessible, and as more students took advantage of the funding opportunity, colleges began charging higher tuition and fees because it meant they wouldn't be on the hook for those loans—the federal government would be.

In fact, colleges now raise tuition more than three times faster than they did before MISAA. The average tuition increase is nearly three times the rate of inflation. The cost of college has increased at an annual rate of 6.8 percent since MISAA, yet over the twelve-year period prior to MISAA, the annual rate was just 1.99 percent. That is an increase of 247.2 percent annually.

This annual increase in college tuition along with the student loan debt crisis is intensified by another issue: the true value of the average wage has stagnated, steadily going down since 1991. The financial benefits of a bachelor's degree have declined at an annual rate of 0.86 percent, because the currency value since 1991 has declined 27.7 percent faster than wages have grown.[3]

The most popular and largest federal student loan is the Federal Stafford Loan, which is a low-cost loan to help students pay for their college tuition. There are two types of Stafford Loans, subsidized and unsubsidized. The interest on subsidized loans is paid by the federal government while the student is in school, and the interest on unsubsidized loans is paid by the student while in school. The interest rate on these loans is fixed at the current rate. The 2021 rate for undergraduate students was 2.75 percent. Both loans have limits depending on dependency status.

In the 1990s Congress created an avenue for parents and graduate students to borrow unlimited amounts of money for education. These are called Parent Plus and Grad Plus loans. Both are unsubsidized federal education loans for parents of dependent undergraduate students and for graduate students, and are available after a student exhausts their eligibility for Federal Stafford Loans.

The dollar limit on a Plus loan is essentially the total cost of tuition, room and board, and personal expenses for as many years as it takes to get the degree. The result of this reckless lending is that millions of parents and graduate degree earners are burdened with loans they cannot afford to repay.

As of 2021, 3.6 million parents and 1.5 million graduate students are in debt from Plus loans that have an interest rate of 6.28 percent, which is significantly higher than other federal student loans.[4] According to an article in the *Wall Street Journal*, the biggest beneficiaries are universities, particularly private and for-profit ones, because they urge students and parents to take out these loans in order to cover tuition shortfalls without any consideration of affordability.[5]

Although lawmakers are well aware of this problem, they aren't doing anything about it.

Congress has repeatedly punted on changing the programs. Among the reasons: resistance to restricting disadvantaged students' access to funds, fear of angering universities, and the fact that the programs—on paper—have historically made money for the government.[6]

Legislatures won't make any changes like capping the amount borrowers can take out or tightening eligibility requirements to ensure that borrowers can repay these loans. Why? Among other reasons, it isn't easy for lawmakers to sell these changes to their constituents, and families typically don't want restrictions on what they can borrow. Additionally, those with hundreds of thousands of dollars in Plus loan debt tend to be more focused on getting the government to forgive their loans than getting the government to limit access to loans for future generations.

In 2018, Rep. Virginia Foxx, chair of the House Committee on Education and the Workforce, tried to pass a bill that would cap both Plus loans. She believed that letting graduate students borrow uncapped amounts of money incentivized universities to continue raising tuition while sending students into debt. Her elected colleagues were worried that the bill would look like they were taking benefits away from their constituents and therefore wasn't worth taking the risk of having such a tough vote when it could be addressed later.[7]

Some lawmakers are aggressively pursuing governmental student loan forgiveness. However, although forgiving student loans would help borrowers who are struggling to pay off their debt, it would be unfair to folks who either paid off their loans already or opted to attend a more affordable, less prestigious college. Student loan deficit is a serious problem for many, yet the majority of people who take out student loans pay them off within twenty years, thereby fulfilling their obligation. Plus, thousands of these selected to attend schools that fit within their financial means.

There's a lot to take in about the student loan crisis, and there are always multiple sides to every debate. Clearly, no one wants to see people suffer for the rest of their lives because they're weighed down by student loan debt, and those who struggled for many years to pay off their debt certainly wouldn't be happy about other people's loans being forgiven when they had to pay it all back.

The simple solution? Avoid the problem by helping your teen choose an affordable college.

Financial Literacy 101

In my twenty-five years as a high school counselor, there was one particular student who impressed me the most. His name was Sal. Sal was not only polite and well-mannered but also a hardworking student who took the most rigorous honors and AP courses and received As in every class he took all four years of high school.

Sal also scored a 1450 on the SAT exam, was swim team captain, participated in many other clubs and activities, and had a part-time job. His parents immigrated from Russia, and Sal would become a first-generation college student. He was a prime candidate to be admitted to some of the nation's top colleges, and he planned to major in mechanical engineering.

One day, late in his senior year, Sal came to my office feeling pretty down. I asked him what was wrong, and he told me that although he was accepted to The College of New Jersey, which was his first choice, he'd received very little scholarship money or student aid.

New Jersey had one of the highest in-state tuitions in the country at around $30,000 a year including room and board, which meant that if Sal chose to go there he would need to assume more than $120,000 in student loans, something he was not willing to do. The cost of his education was his responsibility, and the last thing he wanted was to be burdened with student loans for the next twenty years.

Sal was also accepted to New Jersey Institute of Technology. Although not his first choice, it was an excellent school that would prepare him in mechanical engineering, and they gave him a full academic scholarship. Although Sal could have attended a more "prestigious" school, he made the right financial decision and went to New Jersey Institute of Technology. Given his work ethic, people skills, and emotional intelligence, Sal would have no problem securing a well-paying job after he graduated.

So, why isn't everyone like Sal? Why do so many kids agree to attend colleges they can't afford, even though they can get the same education from one they can afford? For that matter, Why would someone purchase a Mercedes Benz when they could buy a Honda Accord, which is a more reliable car and a quarter of the price? These are excellent questions, ones that Robert Kiyosaki knows well.

Kiyosaki is the author of one of the best financial advice books in history called *Rich Dad Poor Dad*. If you haven't read his book, you should. *Rich Dad Poor Dad* has sold over 32 million copies across more than 109 countries since its release in 1997. The book teaches the difference between working for your money and having your money work for you. It also explains the illusion of wealth and how we assume that the fancy car someone drives is a sign of wealth when it's actually a sign of debt, considering that cars depreciate in value over time.

A perfect example is a friend of mine with a lot of expensive toys. He leases expensive cars and has spent hundreds of thousands of dollars on house renovations and landscaping. About ten years ago, we were having a conversation and finances came up. He said to me, "Tom, I have no idea what I'm going to do about my kids' college or my retirement. I don't have any money saved."

I was shocked, because based on the lifestyle I saw him live, I assumed he was a wealthy guy, but as Richard Kiyosaki points out, wealth isn't the amount of nice things you have; it's the amount of zeros in your bank account.

The Invisible College Degree

I could probably write an entire book about people I know who sent their teenagers to expensive colleges from which they graduated with degrees that weren't tied to a particular profession and were unfortunately useless. Their college tuition became an expense rather than an investment. Other people I know graduated with degrees in certain areas of study that don't even require a degree for employment.

One man's daughter applied to many of the nation's most prestigious colleges her senior year in high school but was denied acceptance. She attended a less prestigious college for two years, did well, and then applied as a transfer student to the University of Pennsylvania (UPenn), which is an Ivy League college. She was accepted.

Two years later, she graduated from UPenn with a degree in Jewish Studies—and currently makes minimum wage working at a local market. The family was very wealthy, so there was no student loan debt to worry about. However, let's imagine that the family wasn't wealthy and took on a massive amount of student loans in order for her to attend

UPenn. This raises some important questions. Number one, what jobs are there in the field of Jewish Studies? Good question. If there are any, what kind of salary could this young woman earn? Would it be enough to pay off all of that debt in a timely manner? Most definitely not. Is it likely that she would be stuck behind the eight ball, financially, for many years? Absolutely.

I'm sure she experienced wonderful things at UPenn, and I'm sure her experience there expanded her intellectual curiosity. However, the question I would ask is this: Is that what college is for? Maybe for some it is, but for most it is not. Higher education is about majoring in a field of study that will lead to a meaningful, well-paying job.

Allow me to put all of this in perspective. As I noted earlier, we currently have a $1.75 trillion student loan crisis that affects 43 million Americans. That can only mean one of two things. Either those individuals went to colleges they couldn't afford or they majored in an area of study that does not pay enough upon employment to be able to pay back those loans.

Furthermore, as I cited earlier, the average tuition increase is three times the rate of inflation, and the financial benefit of a bachelor's degree is declining at an annual rate of 0.86 percent because the currency value has declined 27.7 percent faster than wages have grown. None of it makes financial sense.

Finally, excessive college debt is one of the main stressors for millennials. Many are forced to live with their parents well into their twenties and even thirties because of this. The domino effect from excessive student loan debt causes a delay in marriage, childbearing, home ownership, and retirement savings.

The College "Lost Boys"

Earlier I talked about the young men I counsel whom I call the lost boys. These late teens and early twentysomethings lack direction and motivation, often stemming from marijuana use. Colleges are seeing a similar trend. According to a piece in the *Wall Street Journal*, a generation of American men are giving up on college and feel lost.[8]

Once the predominant group on college campuses, males have now fallen behind females in enrollment rates even though females make up less than half of the college-age population. For the 2020–21 academic year, women made up 60 percent of college students, an all-time high, while men made up just 40 percent. These are excellent advances in equality for women, but there is something going on with young men that we need to explore.

Compared to five years ago, colleges and universities saw a decline of 1.5 million students, and men accounted for 71 percent of that decline. According to Jennifer Delahunty, a college enrollment consultant who was interviewed for the article, "the conventional view on campuses is that men make more money, men hold higher positions, why should we give them a little shove from high school to college?" However, Delahunty believes that the stakes are too high to simply ignore the glaring drop in young men enrolling in college. "If you care about our society, one, and two, if you care about women, you have to care about the boys too. If you have equally educated numbers of men and women that just makes a better society, and it makes it better for women."

College graduates earn more than a million dollars more over their working lives than those with only a high school diploma, though the skyrocketing costs to attend college compared to past generations does make it more risky. According to the article, social science researchers believe there are specific distractions and obstacles to education that weigh more on boys and young men, namely video games, pornography, increased fatherlessness, and overdiagnosis of boyhood restlessness and related medications.

Several young men who dropped out of college and were interviewed for the article said that although they worried about their future, they dropped out anyway with no plan in mind. "I would say I feel hazy. I'm sort of waiting for a light to come on so I figure out what to do next," said one. Another commented, "I don't know what I'm going to do. I just feel lost."

Although men still dominate top positions in finance, politics, and other industries, "female college students are running laps around their male counterparts."[9] For example, at the University of Vermont the school president is a man, as are two-thirds of the campus trustees, yet women made up 80 percent of honors graduates last year in their colleges of arts and sciences. One male student said, "I see a lot of guys that are here for four years to drink beer, smoke weed, hang out, and get a degree." Perhaps this is part of the reason that 70 percent of females at the university graduate in four years compared to just 55 percent of male students.

Current female students also benefit from a valuable support system that was established as women struggled to gain a foothold on college campuses. There are now more than five hundred women's centers at colleges nationwide that help female students succeed, yet very few for men. Though historically males have been the most privileged group on campus with the most resources, perhaps the time has come to create a similar support system for them.

This idea is still not widespread, though some schools such as the University of Oregon have created a collegiate men's center, which offers help for mental and physical health. Hopefully more centers like this will open at other colleges in the near future.

Community College

The good news is that there are plenty of options for all students. If your son or daughter isn't ready to attend a four-year college because of rising costs, lack of maturity, or other reasons, there are alternatives. For example, they can start at a two-year community college and go from there. This way they can experience college at a much lower cost. If college isn't right for them, at least they won't have to break the bank should they drop out of a community college.

Many community colleges across the country provide an excellent education and an excellent opportunity for anyone at a fraction of the cost of name-brand colleges. If a motivated student decides to attend a community college for two years, they can then transfer to a four-year private or public university to finish their remaining two years of college, saving a tremendous amount of money.

In New Jersey, where I live, there's an excellent program called NJ STARS, an initiative that provides high-performing high school students with free tuition to their local community college. NJ STARS students who earn an associate's degree with a cumulative GPA of 3.25 or higher, and have a family income of less than $250,000 per year, are also eligible to continue at one of New Jersey's state universities and earn their bachelor's degree free of charge. Other states and even some cities offer similar programs, and it is something folks should really consider.

Alternatives to the College Degree

According to Jessica Dickler, the college debt crisis is driving more students away from four-year schools. In an article she wrote for CNBC, students are more interested than ever in affordable options.[10] For example, Dickler interviewed twenty-one-year-old Kate Lillemoen, who completed a coding bootcamp offered by an organization called Tech Elevator, which offers intensive in-person and remote learning that helps individuals and companies acquire in-demand technology skills for the modern workforce. Its graduates have a 90 percent employment rate, securing jobs in software development in over four hundred companies nationwide.

Lillemoen is one of them. She decided to leave her four-year college to attend a fourteen-week program with Tech Elevator, and she now works as a software engineer in Columbus, Ohio. Many large employers, including Apple, Bank of America, Google, and IBM, employ graduates of this program. In fact, these companies no longer require four-year college degrees at all. Tech Elevator's fourteen-week program is substantially less expensive than a four-year college degree.

According to Dickler, a recent survey of high school students found that the likelihood of attending a four-year school dropped nearly 20 percent in less than a year—down to 53 percent from 71 percent. That is a staggering number, and it is because of the financial burden that comes with attending a four-year college. Furthermore, the students surveyed were placing more emphasis on career training and post-college employment, and only one-fourth believed that a four-year college degree was the only path to a good job.[11]

In summary, the entire college landscape has changed. What was once an opportunity for young adults to learn a particular profession such as education, accounting, or economics as a means to a gainful, well-paying career has turned into a black hole of debt. Countless teenagers every year are mesmerized by the brand name and prestige that colleges market to them, and they are hoodwinked into agreeing to overinflated tuition costs. Many wind up earning useless degrees, leaving them with massive amounts of debt and no job. From an economic standpoint, it doesn't make sense, and our society needs to do an about-face. From a mental health standpoint, student loan debt can lead to years of anxiety, depression, and hopelessness, which is certainly not something young folks can continue to withstand.

We need to educate our young adults and ourselves about the debt to value ratio a college degree affords. It comes down to basic economics. Look at it like this. Would you encourage your eighteen-year-old to take out a loan to purchase a $300,000 Ferrari? Probably not. Now, let's replace the Ferrari with a private four-year university that also costs $300,000. Would it make sense to encourage your teen to take out loans for that amount to pursue a degree in, say, education, when they can pursue the same degree at a much less expensive college? Of course not.

Finally, one could argue that the tuition cost to attend an Ivy League college isn't fair because it caters to the wealthy. Is it fair that Rolls Royce or Rolex also cater to the rich?

Would buying a Rolls Royce or a Rolex you cannot afford magically make you rich? No. It's the same premise with overpriced colleges. Attending one of them isn't a magic ticket to wealth. Rather, the pathway to success and potential wealth comes down to the hard work you put in while in college and after college.

CHAPTER TIPS

- Teach your teenagers not to get caught up in the college acceptance pressure scheme. Instead, encourage them to work their hardest and find the college that is the right match and right price for them.
- Educate yourself and your children about the value of the colleges they apply to. Research the average starting salaries of students who graduate from those schools, along with the ten-year post-graduate average salary, and compare that to other colleges that are far less expensive.
- Do not get caught up in the game. The sticker on the back of your car advertising the college/colleges your children attend is not a sign of success, the same way that the Mercedes Benz sitting in your neighbor's driveway is not a sign of wealth. It is all a mirage.
- Read *Rich Dad Poor Dad*. It is a simple read and a real wake-up call about how to invest your money wisely. College should be an investment, not a debt liability.

- Open your mind to the value of having your children attend a community college for two years and then transfer to a four-year state college. It may not seem impressive in the eyes of others, but personal wisdom will always prevail over the judgment of others.
- Explore excellent alternatives to a four-year college degree, such as Tech Elevator.

Final Thoughts

Our children haven't changed. The world around them has. We can't turn back the clock and bring back the 1970s and '80s when there seemed to be less chaos in the world, but we can influence the future that our children and grandchildren have. It will take a lot of hard work and a lot of hard parenting. We must identify ways to overcome the societal changes that negatively impact our children's thoughts, beliefs, morals, and lives.

Fellow parents, we are up against a tsunami, a tidal wave of information, pressure, and influences that make their way into our children's malleable minds and often cause confusion, turmoil, and serious mental health issues. It is critical that we spend as much time as we possibly can with our children—quality time—and that we talk with them and teach them about what is right, what is real, and what is just. We cannot relinquish this responsibility to anyone else, whether it be schools, social media influencers, or politicians.

The first step is to get our children out of their bedrooms and into the family room and the outdoors. Outdoor play and involvement with peers are important for their mental and physical health as well as their social-emotional development. Teach your children the art of boredom. Intentional, focused quiet time is the pathway to understanding and knowing oneself and thereby loving oneself. If your child is unruly or oppositional, it is likely that they are either exposed to too much online content that parallels this behavior or accustomed to instant gratification. The best way to delay gratification is to use the word *no*, and use it often.

Substance abuse is another problem that can affect the lives of adolescents. It is normal for teens to feel pressured, want to fit in, and be followers of the crowd. However, we can teach them what it means to be a leader and to do what is right—even if it is not popular. It is our job to talk to them about what it means to be a leader, as it is foundational to character, values, and self-esteem.

We must also lead by example. That means you must have zero tolerance for alcohol and other drugs, including marijuana, regardless of what is allowed in the households of your teenager's friends. Yes, drug overdoses have become a national emergency, and so has childhood obesity.

Childhood obesity is very preventable. Our children need to and are meant to be moving. They are not meant to be sedentary, sitting in front of screens all day. Inexpensive, high-calorie foods are abundant and easily accessible. Fill your refrigerator with fresh fruits and vegetables instead, and make junk food the exception rather than the norm. Doing so is not only good for their physical health but also their mental health.

Your children deserve the best education possible. Yes, they are up against the machines in the classroom and out of the classroom, but if used properly, computer-based learning has its merits. Know what is being taught in your children's school and attend school board meetings. Be a part of your children's education. If your public school does not meet your family's values and beliefs, consider alternatives, many of which are more affordable than you may think.

Finally, applying to college should be an exciting time in your children's lives. Unfortunately it can feel stressful, as our children will likely deal with rejection. Help them understand that the opportunity to attend college is a gift, regardless of where they attend. Also, help them to understand what the true values of attending college are, and that pursuing an alternative path can be good for them. The last thing our children need, or we need, is to be behind the financial eight ball for years to come. College debt is real, and it is a choice.

God bless, and happy parenting!

Acknowledgments

I want to thank my wife, Krista, my son, Matthew, and my daughter, Ashlyn, for their support and encouragement. I thank my parents, my brother and sisters, and my in-laws and friends for always being there. And above all I thank God for blessing me.

Notes

Chapter 1 Mental Freedom

1. Dr. Aric Sigman, "A Movement for Movement: Screen Time, Physical Activity and Sleep: A New Integrated Approach for Children," API, accessed April 13, 2022, https://www.api-play.org/news-events/a-movement-for-movement/.

2. American Academy of Child and Adolescent Psychiatry, "Screen Time and Children," *Facts for Families* 54 (February 2020), https://www.aacap.org/AACAP/Families_and_Youth/Facts_for_Families/FFF-Guide/Children-And-Watching-TV-054.aspx.

3. Nick Kilvert, "Screen Time vs 'Green Time': New Research Suggests Parents Are Right to Nag Kids about Playing Outside," ABC News, September 4, 2020, https://www.abc.net.au/news/science/2020-09-05/screen-time-mental-health-kids-adolescents/12612454.

4. "Kamik Survey: Children Spending 35 Percent Less Time Playing Freely Outside," SGB Media, September 20, 2018, https://sgbonline.com/kamik-survey-childre-spending-35-percent-less-time-playing-freely-outside/.

5. Danielle Cohen, "Why Kids Need to Spend Time in Nature: They May Prefer to Stick to Their Screens, but Here's Why Getting Outdoors Matters," Child Mind Institute, accessed April 13, 2022, https://childmind.org/article/why-kids-need-to-spend-time-in-nature/#full_article.

6. Vanessa Dwyre, "Nature Deficit Disorder and the Need for Environmental Education (Thesis)," Fordham Research Commons, May 8, 2015, https://research.library.fordham.edu/environ_2015/11/.

7. Cohen, "Why Kids Need to Spend Time in Nature."

8. Cohen, "Why Kids Need to Spend Time in Nature."

9. Jean M. Twenge, "Increases in Depression, Self-Harm, and Suicide Among U.S. Adolescents After 2012 and Links to Technology Use: Possible Mechanisms," *Psychiatric Research and Clinical Practice* 2, no. 1 (March 2020), https://www.researchgate.net/publication/340234729_Increases_in _Depression_Self-Harm_and_Suicide_Among_US_Adolescents_After _2012_and_Links_to_Technology_Use_Possible_Mechanisms.

10. Victoria Friedman, "'Locked-In Trauma': Young Children Having Panic Attacks After Playdates," Breitbart, June 22, 2021, https://www.breit bart.com/europe/2021/06/22/locked-in-trauma-young-children-having -panic-attacks-playdates/.

11. "How Young People's Social Anxiety Has Worsened in the Pandemic," DNYUZ, September 27, 2021, https://dnyuz.com/2021/09/27 /how-young-peoples-social-anxiety-has-worsened-in-the-pandemic/.

12. A. W. Geiger and Leslie Davis, "A Growing Number of American Teenagers—Particularly Girls—Are Facing Depression," Pew Research Center, July 12, 2019, https://www.pewresearch.org/fact-tank/2019/07/12 /a-growing-number-of-american-teenagers-particularly-girls-are-facing -depression/.

13. Deepa Shivaram, "Pediatricians Say the Mental Health Crisis among Kids Has Become a National Emergency," NPR, October 20, 2021, https://www.npr.org/2021/10/20/1047624943/pediatricians-call -mental-health-crisis-among-kids-a-national-emergency.

14. Virginia Yurich, "About Us," 1000 Hours Outside, accessed April 13, 2022, https://www.1000hoursoutside.com/about-us.

15. Head over to 1000hoursoutside.com to learn more. Thank you, Ginny and Josh!

16. David Wright and Hanna Siegel, "Bikes, Balls in Class: How Phys Ed Transformed One School," ABC News, April 14, 2010, https://abcnews .go.com/WN/exercise-school-leads-learning/story?id=10371315.

17. Wright and Siegel, "Bikes, Balls in Class."

Chapter 2 Social Nutrition

1. Damon E. Jones, Mark Greenberg, and Max Crowley, "Early Social-Emotional Functioning and Public Health: The Relationship between Kindergarten Social Competence and Future Wellness," *American Journal of Public Health* 105, no. 11 (November 2015): 2283–90, https://ajph .aphapublications.org/doi/10.2105/AJPH.2015.302630.

2. Stuart Brown, "Play Deprivation Can Damage Early Child Development," *Child & Family Blog*, October 2018, https://childandfamilyblog .com/play-deprivation-early-child-development/.

3. Brown, "Play Deprivation Can Damage Early Child Development."
4. Brown, "Play Deprivation Can Damage Early Child Development."
5. Nick Triggle, "Covid: The Devastating Toll of the Pandemic on Children," BBC News, January 30, 2021, https://www.bbc.com/news/health-55863841.
6. Triggle, "Covid."
7. Margery Smelkinson, Leslie Bienen, and Jeanne Noble, "The Case Against Masks at School," *Atlantic*, January 26, 2022, https://www.the atlantic.com/ideas/archive/2022/01/kids-masks-schools-weak-science/621133/.
8. Kristen Rogers, "Does Mask Wearing Harm Your Child's Development? Experts Weigh In," CNN, August 11, 2021, https://www.cnn.com/2021/08/11/health/masks-child-development-effects-covid-pandemic-wellness/index.html.
9. Rogers, "Does Mask Wearing Harm?"
10. University of Edinburgh, "COVID-19 Less Deadly and Causes Milder Symptoms in Children, UK Study Finds," ScienceDaily, August 28, 2020, https://www.sciencedaily.com/releases/2020/08/200827205417.htm.
11. Jay Donovan, "The Average Age for a Child Getting Their First Smartphone Is Now 10.3 Years," TechCrunch, May 19, 2016, https://techcrunch.com/2016/05/19/the-average-age-for-a-child-getting-their-first-smartphone-is-now-10-3-years/.
12. Meeri Kim, "Boredom's Link to Mental Illnesses, Brain Injuries and Dysfunctional Behaviors," *Washington Post*, July 17, 2021, https://www.washingtonpost.com/health/boredom-mental-health-disconnected/2021/07/16/c367cd30-9d6a-11eb-9d05-ae06f4529ece_story.html.Behavior."
13. Kim, "Boredom's Link to Mental Illnesses."
14. Julie Jargon, "Teen Girls Are Developing Tics. Doctors Say TikTok Could Be a Factor," *Wall Street Journal*, October 19, 2021, https://www.wsj.com/articles/teen-girls-are-developing-tics-doctors-say-tiktok-could-be-a-factor-11634389201.
15. Jargon, "Teen Girls Are Developing Tics."
16. Study Finds with Georgia Lambert, "Having Deep Conversations with Strangers Can Improve Our Well-Being," Study Finds, October 4, 2021, https://www.studyfinds.org/deep-conversations-strangers/.

Chapter 3 Fear-Filled Nation

1. Erin Digitale, "Stanford Study Finds Stronger One-Way Fear Signals in Brains of Anxious Kids," Stanford Medicine, April 21, 2020,

https://med.stanford.edu/news/all-news/2020/04/stanford-study-finds
-stronger-one-way-fear-signals-in-brains-of-.html.
  2. Digitale, "Stanford Study Finds Stronger One-Way Fear Signals."
  3. COVID-19 Mental Disorders Collaborators, "Global Prevalence and Burden of Depressive and Anxiety Disorders in 204 Countries and Territories in 2020 Due to the COVID-19 Pandemic," *The Lancet* 398, no. 10312 (October 8, 2021): 1700–1712, https://www.thelancet.com/journals/lancet/article/PIIS0140-6736(21)02143-7/fulltext.
  4. Will Fulton, "6 Reasons Your Doctor Wants You to Stop Using WebMD," *Thrillist,* June 19, 2015, https://www.thrillist.com/culture/do-doctors-hate-webmd-negatives-of-using-webmd-what-do-doctors-think-about-webmd.
  5. As quoted in Melaina Juntti, "Why Are Kids Easily Scared? Because That's How Brain Development Works," Fatherly, March 2, 2021, https://www.fatherly.com/health-science/why-are-kids-easily-scared-brain-development/.

Chapter 4 Behavior and Conduct Issues

  1. Kalyn Belsha, "Stress and Short Tempers: Schools Struggle with Behavior as Students Return," Chalkbeat, September 27, 2021, https://www.chalkbeat.org/2021/9/27/22691601/student-behavior-stress-trauma-return/.
  2. Brooke Baitinger and Scott Travis, "'We Are Scared Every Day': Student Fights and Assaults on Teachers Trouble Florida Schools Amid Pandemic," *Florida Sun-Sentinel,* November 26, 2021, https://www.sun-sentinel.com/news/education/fl-ne-schools-fights-violence-pandemic-20211126-ey2blaezofai7cbodky4xvzajy-story.html.
  3. Baitinger and Travis, "'We Are Scared Every Day.'"
  4. "Oppositional Defiant Disorder (ODD) in Children," Johns Hopkins Medicine, accessed April 26, 2021, https://www.hopkinsmedicine.org/health/conditions-and-diseases/oppositional-defiant-disorder.
  5. Danielle Wallace, "Crime Forces Jersey Shore Town to Close Beach, Boardwalk Early," Fox News, July 12, 2021, https://www.foxnews.com/us/jersey-shore-town-crime-beach-boardwalk-close-early.
  6. Avery Hartmans, "A Harvard Psychologist Explains the Rise in Passengers Getting Violent on Airplanes and Customers Abusing Retail Workers: People Have Reached 'A Boiling Point,'" *Insider,* July 24, 2021, https://www.businessinsider.com/violence-on-airplanes-in-stores-explained-harvard-psychologist-2021-7.
  7. Leslie Josephs, "Delta Asks the Justice Department to Put Unruly Passengers on a 'No-Fly' List," CNBC, February 5, 2022, https://

www.cnbc.com/2022/02/05/delta-asks-the-justice-department-to-put
-unruly-travelers-on-a-no-fly-list.html.

8. Anna Lembke, "Digital Addictions Are Drowning Us in Dopamine:
Rising Rates of Depression and Anxiety in Wealthy Countries like the U.S.
May Be a Result of Our Brains Getting Hooked on the Neurotransmitter
Associated with Pleasure," *Wall Street Journal*, August 13, 2021, https://
www.wsj.com/articles/digital-addictions-are-drowning-us-in-dopamine
-11628861572.

9. George Barna, "New Insights into the Generation of Growing Influence: Millennials in America," *Foundations of Freedom*, October 2021
(Phoenix: Arizona Christian University Cultural Research Center), 42,
https://www.arizonachristian.edu/wp-content/uploads/2021/10/George
-Barna-Millennial-Report-2021-FINAL-Web.pdf.

10. Barna, "New Insights into the Generation of Growing Influence," 48.

11. Barna, "New Insights into the Generation of Growing Influence,"
74, 24, 76, 18, 11.

Chapter 5 Substance Abuse

1. Patrick Lynch, "Average THC Strength Over Time: A 50-Year Look
at Marijuana Potency," *Way of Leaf* (blog), November 1, 2021, https://
wayofleaf.com/blog/average-thc-content-over-the-years.

2. Newport Academy, "What Is Scromiting and Why Are More Teens
Developing It?," Newport Academy, September 1, 2021, https://www
.newportacademy.com/resources/treatment/teen-scromiting/.

3. Newport Academy, "What Is Scromiting?"

4. National Institute on Drug Abuse, "Overdose Death Rates," National Institutes of Health, January 20, 2022, https://nida.nih.gov/drug
-topics/trends-statistics/overdose-death-rates.

5. National Institute on Drug Abuse, "Overdose Death Rates."

6. "A Time of Crisis for the Opioid Epidemic in the USA," *The Lancet*
398, no. 10297 (July 24, 2021): 277, https://www.thelancet.com/journals
/lancet/article/PIIS0140-6736(21)01653-6/fulltext.

7. U.S. Customs and Border Protection, "CBP Officers at South Texas
Ports of Entry Post Significant Increases in Fentanyl, Cocaine Seized in
FY 2021," U.S. Customs and Border Protection, January 5, 2022, https://
www.cbp.gov/newsroom/local-media-release/cbp-officers-south-texas
-ports-entry-post-significant-increases-0#.

8. Robert Sherman and Char'Nese Turner, "1,066% Increase in Fentanyl Seizures at US Border," News Nation, February 3, 2022, https://www
.newsnationnow.com/us-news/immigration/1066-increase-in-fentanyl
-seizures-at-us-border/.

Chapter 6 Obesity and Body Image

1. The Nutrition Source, "Sugary Drinks," Harvard T. H. Chan School of Public Health, accessed April 27, 2022, https://www.hsph.harvard.edu/nutritionsource/healthy-drinks/sugary-drinks/.

2. Centers for Disease Control and Prevention, "Childhood Obesity Facts," Overweight and Obesity, April 5, 2021, https://www.cdc.gov/obesity/data/childhood.html.

3. Eric Schlosser, *Fast Food Nation: The Dark Side of the All-American Meal* (New York: Houghton Mifflin Harcourt, 2002), 54.

4. Schlosser, *Fast Food Nation*, 54.

5. Jennifer L. Harris et al., "Fast Food Facts 2021," UCONN Rudd Center for Food Policy and Obesity, June 2021, https://media.ruddcenter.uconn.edu/PDFs/FACTS2021.pdf.

6. All Kids Bike, accessed May 5, 2022, https://allkidsbike.org/research-and-resources/.

7. Dawn Morrison, "Dal Study Shows Importance of Physical Activity and Social Connection for Kids during COVID-19 Lockdowns," Dalhousie University News, May 10, 2021, https://www.dal.ca/faculty/health/news-events/news/2021/05/10/dal_study_shows_importance_of_physical_activity_and_social_connection_for_kids_during_covid_19_lockdowns.html.

8. Morrison, "Dal Study Shows Importance."

9. Georgia Wells, Jeff Horitz, and Deepa Seetharaman, "Facebook Knows Instagram Is Toxic for Teen Girls, Company Documents Show," *Wall Street Journal*, September 14, 2021, https://www.wsj.com/articles/facebook-knows-instagram-is-toxic-for-teen-girls-company-documents-show-11631620739.

10. Althea Chang-Cook, "Where to Turn When Social Media Worsens Body Image Issues," *Consumer Reports*, November 8, 2021, https://www.consumerreports.org/mental-health/where-to-turn-when-social-media-worsens-body-image-issues-a8010869684/.

11. Chang-Cook, "Where to Turn."

12. Julia F. Taylor and Sara Groff Stephens, "The COVID-19 Pandemic Increased Eating Disorders among Young People—But the Signs Aren't What Parents Might Expect," PhillyVoice, November 13, 2021, https://www.phillyvoice.com/eating-disorders-signs-boys-lgbtq-anorexia-bulimia-binge-eating/.

Chapter 7 School and Learning

1. Kerry McDonald, "Cities Lead the Way in (Another) Massive Fall Exodus from US Public Schools," FEE Stories, October 12, 2021, https://

fee.org/articles/cities-lead-the-way-in-another-massive-fall-exodus-from
-us-public-schools/.

2. McDonald, "Cities Lead the Way."

3. As quoted in Robert Farrington, "How Covid-19 Boosted Private
School Enrollment Forever," *Forbes*, June 8, 2021, https://www.forbes
.com/sites/robertfarrington/2021/06/08/how-covid-19-boosted-private
-school-enrollment-forever/?sh=16f27a3b96fc.

4. Farrington, "How Covid-19 Boosted Private School Enrollment."

5. Lauren Camera, "Catholic Schools Find Silver Lining in Pandemic:
First Enrollment Increase in Two Decades," *U.S. News*, February 16,
2022, https://www.usnews.com/news/education-news/articles/2022-02
-16/catholic-schools-find-silver-lining-in-pandemic-first-enrollment-in
crease-in-two-decades.

6. Jason O'Day, "Homeschooling Increases in North Dakota by More
Than 1,500 Students from 2019–2020 School Year," *The Dickinson Press*,
November 3, 2021, https://www.thedickinsonpress.com/news/home
schooling-increases-in-north-dakota-by-more-than-1-500-students-from
-2019-2020-school-year.

7. Stephen Duvall, "Why Will Parents Likely Continue to Homeschool
During the 2021–22 School Year?," Home School Legal Defense Association, August 10, 2021, https://hslda.org/post/why-will-parents-likely
-continue-to-homeschool-during-the-2021-22-school-year.

8. Duvall, "Why Will Parents Likely Continue to Homeschool?"

Chapter 8 College Admissions Pressure and Debt

1. Melanie Hanson, "Student Loan Debt Crisis," Education Data
Initiative, updated January 5, 2022, https://educationdata.org/student
-loan-debt-crisis.

2. Hanson, "Student Loan Debt Crisis."

3. Hanson, "Student Loan Debt Crisis."

4. Ayelet Sheffey, "3.6 Million Parents Use the Most Expensive Federal
Student Loan to Pay for Their Kids' College. Here's Why It Can Push
Off Retirement," *Insider*, October 4, 2021, https://www.businessinsider
.com/what-are-parent-plus-loans-student-debt-most-expensive-2021-10.

5. Rebecca Ballhaus and Andrea Fuller, "Why Washington Won't Fix
Student Debt Plans That Overload Families," *Wall Street Journal*, December 8, 2021, https://www.wsj.com/articles/college-university-student
-debt-parent-grad-plus-loans-congress-school-borrowing-11638930489.

6. Ballhaus and Fuller, "Why Washington Won't Fix Student Debt Plans."

7. Ballhaus and Fuller, "Why Washington Won't Fix Student Debt
Plans."

8. Douglas Belkin, "A Generation of American Men Give Up on College: 'I Just Feel Lost,'" *Wall Street Journal*, September 6, 2021, https://www.wsj.com/articles/college-university-fall-higher-education-men-women-enrollment-admissions-back-to-school-11630948233.

9. Belkin, "A Generation of American Men Give Up on College."

10. Jessica Dickler, "College Debt Crisis Drives More Students Away from Four-Year Schools," CNBC, September 5, 2021, https://www.cnbc.com/2021/09/05/college-debt-crisis-drives-more-students-away-from-four-year-schools.html.

11. Dickler, "College Debt Crisis Drives More Students Away."

About the Author

Thomas Kersting is a nationally renowned psychotherapist and retired high school counselor. He appears regularly on popular talk shows and news shows, and he has also hosted television series and shows for A&E Network, National Geographic Channel, Food Network, and Oprah's Wellness Network.

CONNECT WITH TOM

TOMKERSTING.COM

 TomKersting   ▮f ThomasKersting

Break Free of the Control Devices Have over You and Your Family

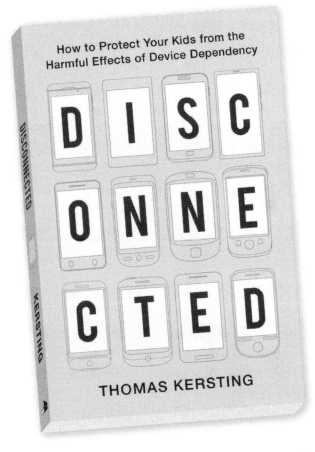

How to Protect Your Kids from the Harmful Effects of Device Dependency

DISCONNECTED

DISCONNECTED

KERSTING

THOMAS KERSTING

In *Disconnected*, psychotherapist and parenting expert Thomas Kersting offers a comprehensive look at how devices have altered the way our children grow up, behave, learn, and connect with their families and friends. Based on the latest studies on the connection between screen time and neuroplasticity, as well as the growing research on acquired ADHD and anxiety, *Disconnected* presents a better way to move forward.

Connect with **BakerBooks**
Relevant. Intelligent. Engaging.

Sign up for announcements about new and upcoming titles at

BakerBooks.com/SignUp

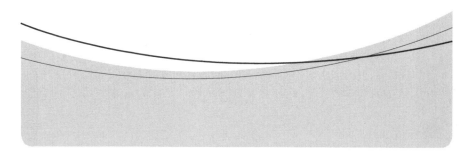

@ReadBakerBooks